CANTERBURY ARCHAEOLOGICAL TRUST OCCASIONAL

EXCAVATIONS AT DOWNLANDS, WALMER, KENT

by

Crispin Jarman

with

Robin Bendrey, Lynne Bevan, Barbara McNee,
Ruth Pelling and Andrew Savage

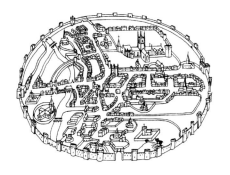

2010 Produced by Canterbury Archaeological Trust Ltd
Printed in UK by parkers digital press, Canterbury

ISBN 978-1-870545-18-1
British Library Cataloguing-in-Publication Data
A catalogue record for this book is available from the British Library

Contents

List of figures

List of plates

List of tables

Summary

Between October 2004 and May 2005 Canterbury Archaeological Trust undertook a programme of excavation on land at Downlands, Walmer, Kent. This work, in advance of construction of housing on a 1.2 hectare site, revealed the presence of prehistoric and Romano-British activity.

The prehistoric occupation commenced in the late Bronze Age and continued up to the early middle Iron Age, perhaps coming to an end in the middle or late fourth century BC. Settlement in the prehistoric period was characterised by intensive pitting bounded to the north by an east–west aligned ditch. The pitting could only be partially sampled within the constraints of time and funding, but sufficient was excavated to characterise the nature of the pits and to provide dating for the activity. The function of individual pits that comprise these complexes is hard to determine. The pits were of varied form, size and depth and it is difficult to associate features spatially or typologically. There is little evidence for refuse disposal within their fills and while the earlier features may have been quarry pits, extracting brickearth, the majority must have served other functions.

Although no prehistoric structures were identified, a small quantity of domestic waste suggests the proximity of habitation. The focus of settlement probably lay under the field to the south of the development. The intensity of the pitting indicates that occupation was on a fairly large scale and/or extended over a considerable period of time; it may also indicate zoning of activities.

The site was reoccupied in the early Roman period, probably not long after the conquest. A sequence of boundary ditches aligned east–west across the site appears to have marked the northern extent of settlement, separating peripheral activity on its edge from fields lying to the north of the site. The isolated burials of a child and of a horse, thought to be Roman in date, lay a short distance to the south of the boundary along with a number of other features.

Towards the end of the second century or early in the third century the earlier features were buried beneath a soil horizon formed by a combination of redeposited occupation material and colluvium. This horizon may represent intentional levelling of the area, though not necessarily in one single event and colluviation may have played its part. Set into the soil horizon were the flint footings of a large aisled building, over 13m wide and probably twice that in length, extending south of the excavation. No floors or related deposits survived within the building. The only associated feature was a ditch, 10m to the east of and parallel to the east wall of the building, extending 15m before turning east along the alignment of the earlier, buried, boundary ditches.

As with the earlier occupation it appears that the excavation picked up the northern periphery of occupation focused to the south of the development. The nature of the settlement is not clear from the evidence; the pottery suggests no more than a native settlement or farmstead. However the presence of a large aisled building in the later phase may indicate a more substantial settlement, perhaps indicating the presence of a Roman villa to the south. In this context it is suggested that the aisled building was probably a barn or other ancillary building, rather than a residence. Evidence for cereal processing associated with the structure supports this conclusion and might possibly indicate that brewing took place at the site.

Acknowledgements

The excavation was commissioned by the developer, Abbey Developments Limited and thanks are extended to Roger Jones, contracts manager, for his involvement in the project. Thanks are also due to Peal Construction for their occasional loan of plant and their helpful co-operation in working around the archaeological field team on what was a confined site with a tight time schedule.

Crispin Jarman directed both the evaluation and excavation and he would like to thank all Trust staff who worked at Downlands, particularly Grant Shand who took charge in his absence. Jon Rady and Peter Clark provided helpful advice during the excavation and post-excavation stages of work respectively and Keith Parfitt is thanked for sharing his extensive local knowledge. Simon Mason of Kent County Council's Heritage Conservation Group is thanked for his assistance throughout.

Dr Enid Allison conducted initial palaeo-environmental processing and organised specialist reports and Yvonne Heath examined the human skeleton. Thanks are extended to them and to all specialist contributors for assistance in producing this report amongst whom Barbara McNee would like to thank Dr David Williams (University of Southampton) and Dr Sandy Budden, a research fellow at the University of Southampton and professional potter, for their helpful comments.

Excavation drawings were prepared by Crispin Jarman and Mark Duncan. Finds were illustrated by Barbara McNee. The report was copy edited by Jane Elder and prepared for print by Mark Duncan and Jane Elder.

Plate 1. The development site from the south corner.

1

Introduction

Background

Between October 2004 and May 2005 Canterbury Archaeological Trust undertook an archaeological excavation on land at Downlands in Walmer, Kent (Fig 1). The work, commissioned by Abbey Developments Limited, was conducted in advance of construction of thirty-seven houses. The excavation was preceded by a programme of archaeological evaluation, conducted in August 2003 and September 2004, which indicated the presence of Romano-British activity confined to the south-west corner of the site (Jarman 2003; 2004).

Site location

The 1.2 hectare site is located on the south edge of Walmer, some 50m east of the A258 (Dover Road) and less than 1km from the east Kent coast (NGR 636770 149700) (Figs 2 and 3). To the south lie open fields, while to the north the site is bounded by houses and gardens. Walmer is located to the south of Deal, at the foot of the North Downs, where the latter meet the English Channel. To the north is the Lydden valley, the Sandwich and Pegwell bays and then the Isle of Thanet at a distance of some 13km. To the south and west of Walmer are the North Downs, rising to the scarp some 17km distant. North of the site is the Wantsum channel, formerly a sea passage between the Isle of Thanet and the mainland.

Geology and topography

The underlying solid geology of the area is Cretaceous Upper Chalk, locally overlain by drift deposits of Head Brickearth (British Geological Survey 1:50,000 Series Dover Sheet 290). Thanet Beds sands outcrop 5km to the north-west of the site and to the north a coastal plain is formed by Dry Valley and Nailbourne Deposits, sand and gravel and Marine Beach Deposits (Fig 4). During the evaluation and excavation Head Brickearth was observed across the north

Plate 2. The Downs to the south of the site with the Roman building in the middle ground.

of the site, with underlying chalk exposed in several places. In the centre and south of the excavation, deposits of clay, gravel, brickearth and chalk were encountered (identified as solifluxion deposits) apparently filling a shallow hollow or valley head extending eastward across the site. Colluvial deposits overlay the entire area, varying in depth from 0.3–0.5m in the west to over 0.8m in the east.

Downlands is situated between the 35 and 40m contours on a gently sloping, north-east facing plateau above a steep drop to the foot of the downs, some 600m to the north-east (Fig 5). To the south and west the ground rises steadily to a wide, open rolling landscape, while to the east the hills meet the sea forming low chalk cliffs. Immediately to the west the land drops into a broad gentle valley leading into the Lydden valley and to the east into a steeper valley opening onto the coast at Deal.

The site itself has been subject to a significant degree of disturbance in recent years. The centre and east of the site was truncated by the formation of a level terrace, probably in the nineteenth or early twentieth century, leaving a 15m wide strip of undisturbed ground to the south and a 50m wide strip to the west (Fig 3). At its deepest the cut for this terracing has removed up to 1m of material, mainly colluvium, but also some archaeological deposits.

Downlands commands a clear view to the north across the east mouth of the Wantsum channel to the Isle of Thanet and is sheltered from the prevailing weather by rolling hills to its south-west. The landscape, presumably partially wooded in the prehistoric and Roman periods, would have provided well drained sheltered areas for fields and a good source of timber for building and fuel. To the north the site would have overlooked marshy ground lying at the foot of the North Downs in the area now occupied by Deal and to the north-west around the mouth of the Lydden valley. The land now occupied by marsh and sand dunes between Deal and Sandwich, known as the Sandhills, would in the prehistoric period probably have been covered by the sea, forming a wide mouth to the Wantsum channel.

The shingle spit, which now extends *c* 8–9km north from Deal, protecting the area to its west from the sea, has led to the formation of a low lying marshy coastal plain. The date at which the spit began to form is not known, but Keith Parfitt reviewing the archaeological data from the Sandhills draws attention to a number of isolated finds from the area and to an occupation site of Roman date at Dickson's Corner, Worth (Parfitt 1982). Parfitt also notes the general absence of prehistoric material, but that the significance of this in dating the spit is uncertain. He concludes that the spit was already well established in the early Roman period and that the area was clearly being occupied or at least exploited at this time. The full extent of the spit and the state of the marsh to its west are, he notes, still uncertain.

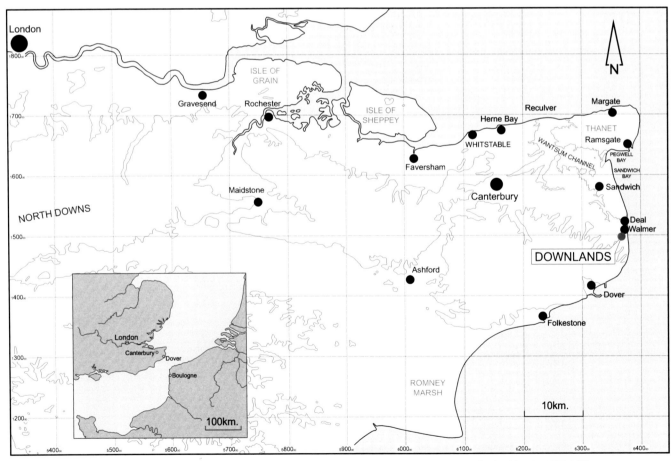

Fig 1. Plan of Kent showing location of the site, major towns and land over 60m with inset plan of south-east England (scale 1:625,000).

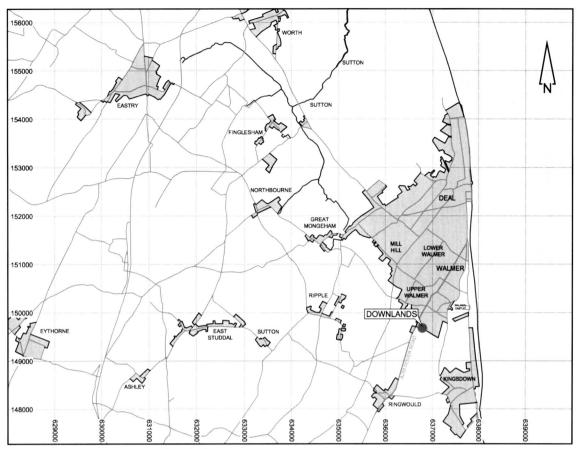

Fig 2. Present day settlement around Downlands.

Excavation strategy

Evaluation trenching had indicated the presence of Romano-British activity in the south-west corner of the development, but had failed to determine its nature. It was therefore decided to excavate a trench, measuring 60 by 35m (c 2100m^2) in this corner of the site (Fig 6). The trench exposed the northern limit of a Romano-British soil horizon cut by a ditch and foundations of a building, all extending to the south of the development. To the north prehistoric pits and ditches were identified cutting the Head Brickearth.

The exposed features were investigated and several trenches were machined through the Romano-British soil (Trenches 15–20, Fig 7) in order to make a rapid record of the deposit and to determine the extent of earlier activity beneath. The Romano-British soil was then removed by machine, in a reduced area (c 915m^2) (Fig 7), corresponding to house plots and gardens. This exposed a poorly differentiated surface formed by intercutting pits and colluvium with little undisturbed ground evident.

Sample excavation of these deposits was further confined to the footprints of buildings and their front gardens. The pit complexes were investigated in Trenches 16–20 and in a series of hand-excavated interventions (Sondages 1–8), representing a c 22 per cent sample of the reduced excavation area (Fig 7). The aim was to create a series of sections running east–west and north–south across the site in order to

obtain representative profiles through the pitting and to date and characterise the activity represented (Figs 9–16).

The stratigraphic record

Survival of the stratigraphic record was exceptional due to the depth of colluvial overburden (Figs 8–16). Few modern disturbances had penetrated this and only a substantial linear feature traversing the site from east–west had caused damage to the sequence. The complexity of the archaeology presented its own problems. The intensity of pitting was such that continued reworking of the soils had led to the formation of an undifferentiated surface in which few individual pits or ditches could be identified. Many of the pits and deposits were only identified in section within the interventions and so proper stratigraphic excavation was compromised. The potential for artefactual contamination was high, both during formation and excavation of the deposits, and so the dating of individual features is to some extent insecure. Furthermore the potential for contamination of soil samples, particularly of prehistoric features is high.

During stratigraphic analysis of the site record associated deposits and cuts were grouped together and assigned to a numbered group sequence. These groups have been retained for use in the discussion below and are referred to by number prefixed by the letter G. Individual deposits and cuts are referred to in the text by the context number assigned in the field.

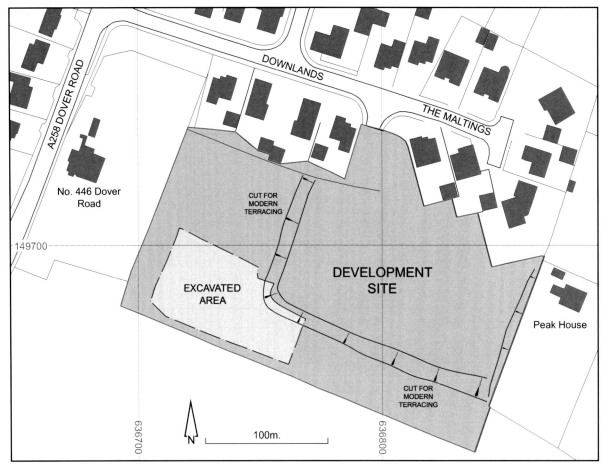

Fig 3. Detail location of the development site showing the position of the excavation in the south-west corner and the modern terracing of the north-east part of the site.

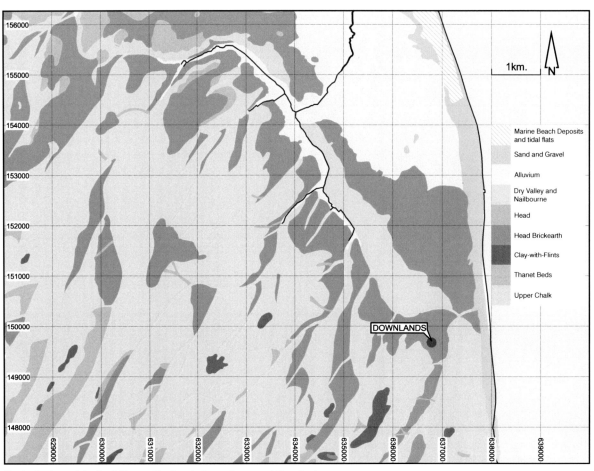

Fig 4. Geology of the North Downs dip slope in the region around Downlands.

4

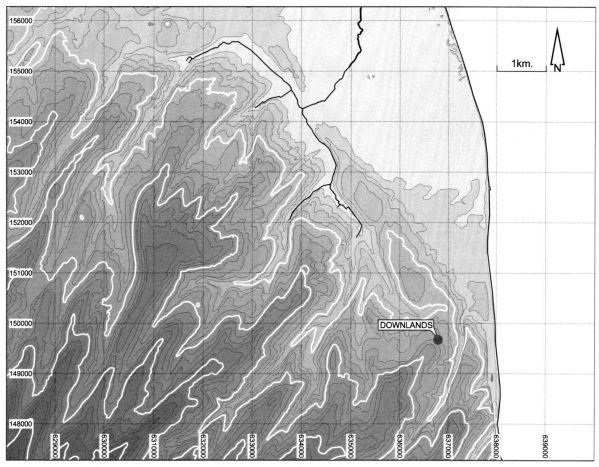

Fig 5. Contour map of the North Downs dip slope in the region around Downlands.

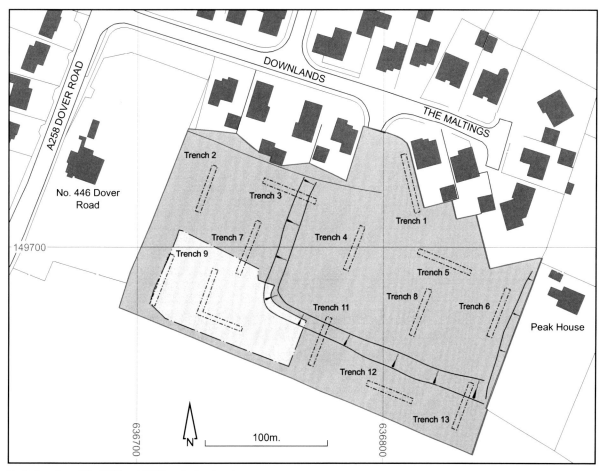

Fig 6. Location of the 2003 and 2004 evaluation trenches.

5

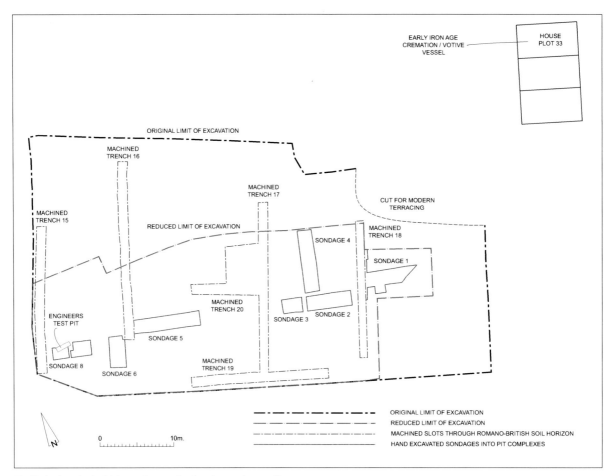

Fig 7. Archaeological interventions and reduced area of excavation.

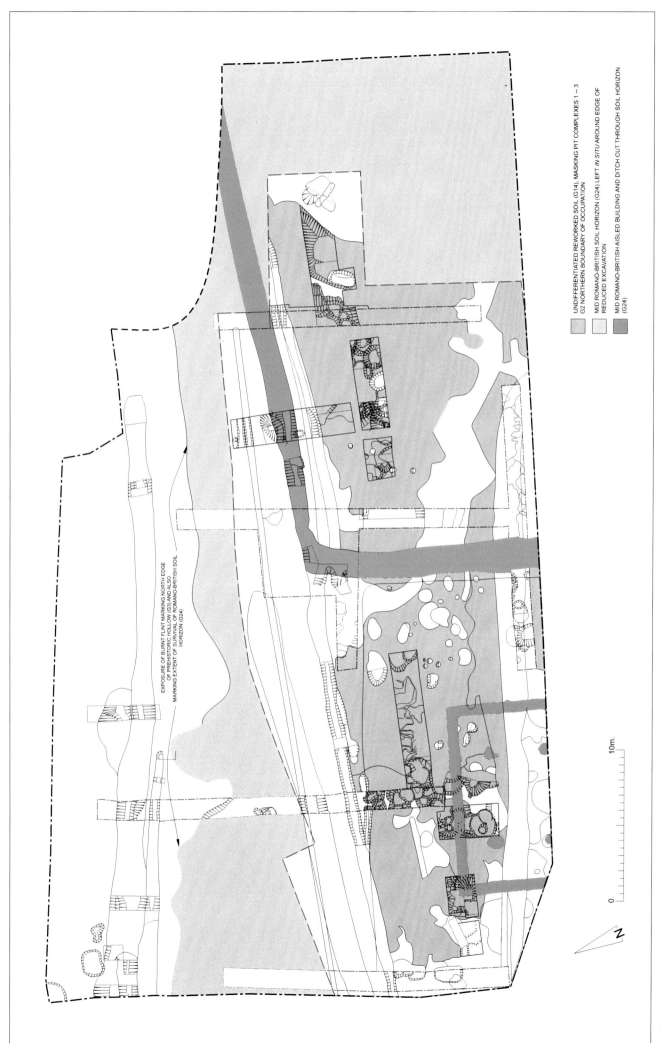

UNDIFFERENTIATED REWORKED SOIL (G14), MASKING PIT COMPLEXES 1 – 3
G2 NORTHERN BOUNDARY OF OCCUPATION

MID ROMANO-BRITISH SOIL HORIZON (G24) LEFT *IN SITU* AROUND EDGE OF
REDUCED EXCAVATION

MID ROMANO-BRITISH AISLED BUILDING AND DITCH CUT THROUGH SOIL HORIZON
(G24)

EXPOSURE OF BURNT FLINT MARKING NORTH EDGE
OF PREHISTORIC HOLLOW (G3) AND ALSO
MARKING EXTENT OF SURVIVAL OF ROMANO-BRITISH SOIL
HORIZON (G24)

0   10m.

N

Fig 8. Unphased plan of all excavated features showing interventions and unexcavated areas of soil deposits G14 and G24.

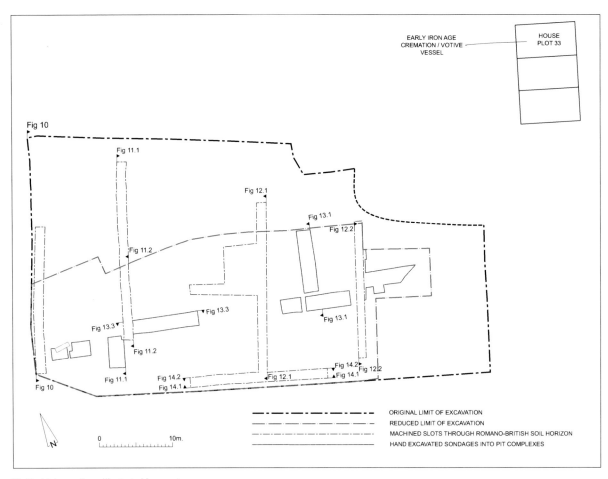

Fig 9. Main sections illustrated in report.

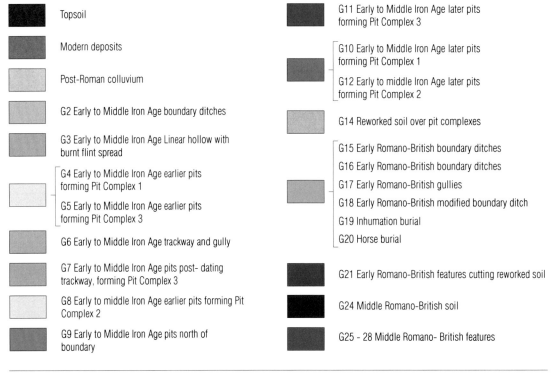

Key to sections.

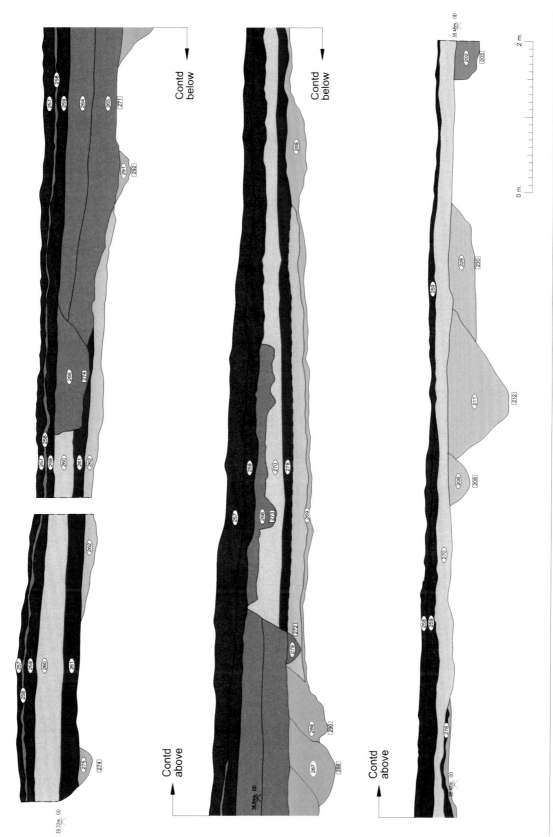

Fig 10. Western limit of excavation (east facing section), showing depth of colluvial overburden and modern disturbances.

9

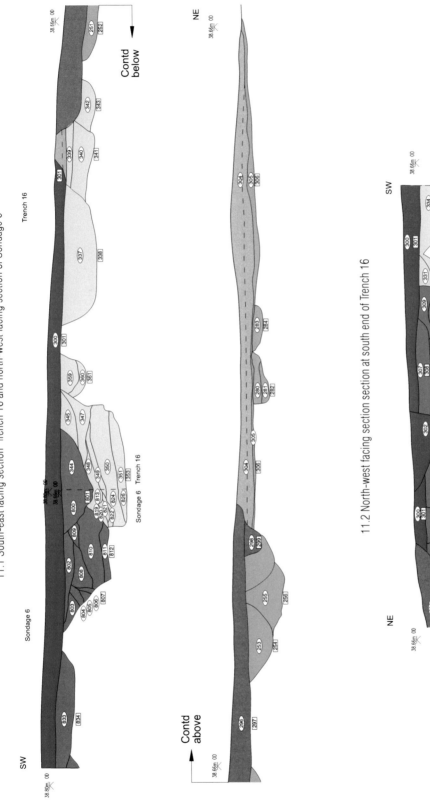

11.1 South-east facing section Trench 16 and north-west facing section of Sondage 6

11.2 North-west facing section section at south end of Trench 16

Fig 11. Trench 16, south-east and north-west facing sections; Sondage 6, north-west facing section showing pit complex 1 sealed beneath the Romano-British soil horizon.

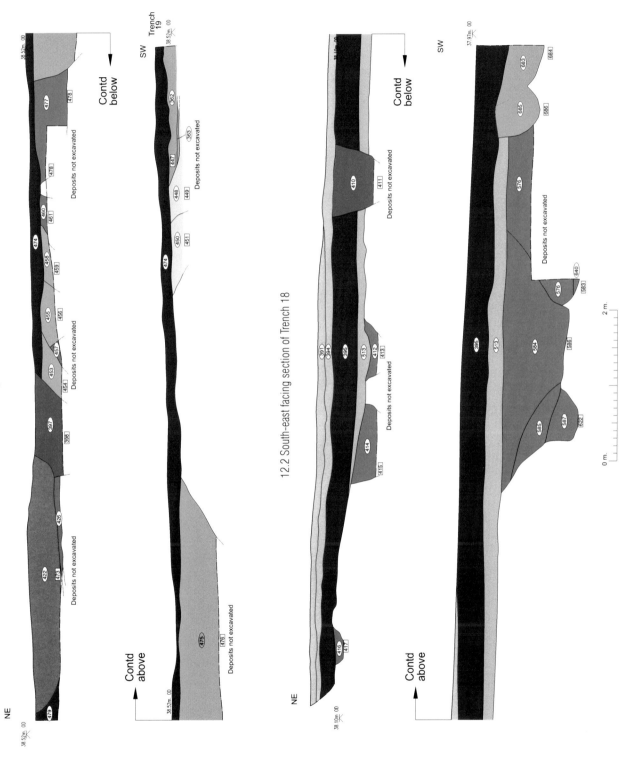

12.1 North-west facing section of Trench 17

12.2 South-east facing section of Trench 18

Fig 12. Trench 17, south-west facing section; Trench 18, north-east facing section.

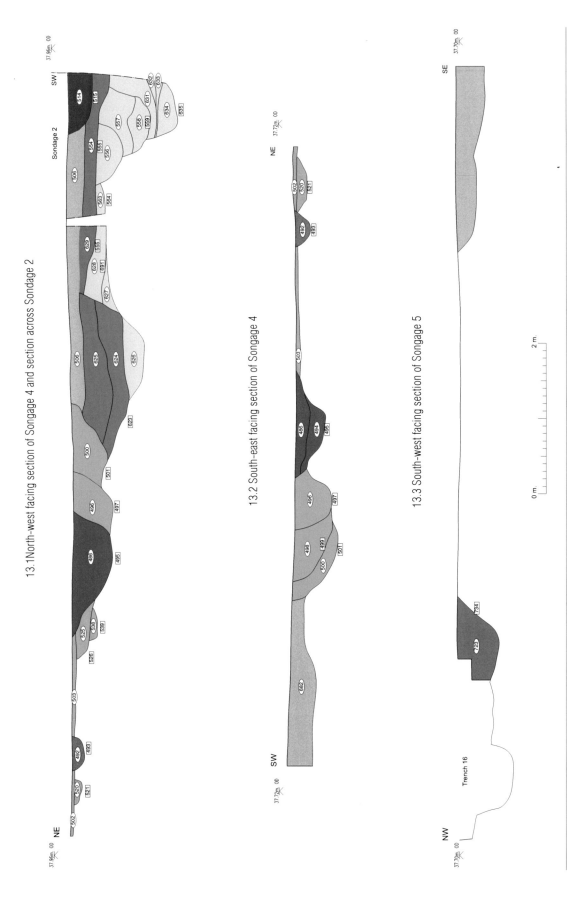

Fig 13. Sondage 4, north-west and south-east facing sections; Sondage 2, north-west facing section showing pit complex 2 and Roman ditches; Sondage 5, south-west facing section.

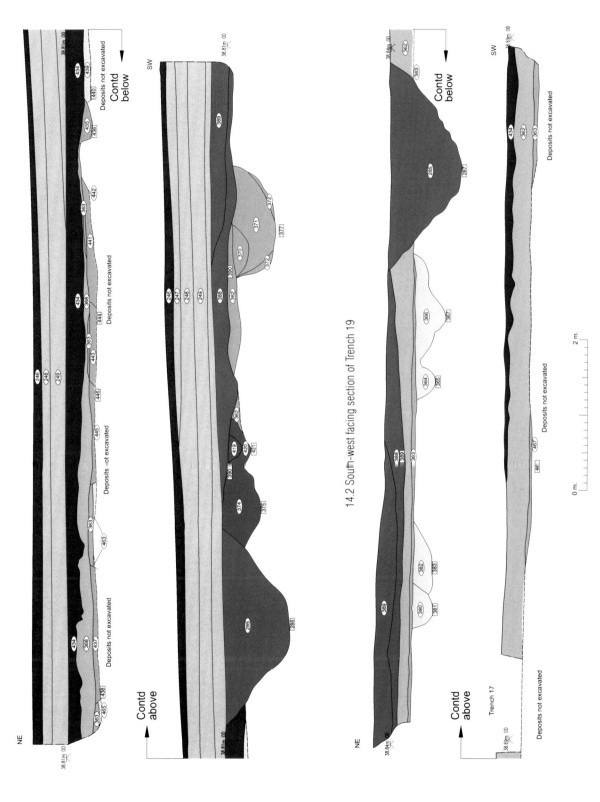

Fig 14. Trench 19, north-east facing section showing depth of colluvial overburden and south-west facing section.

13

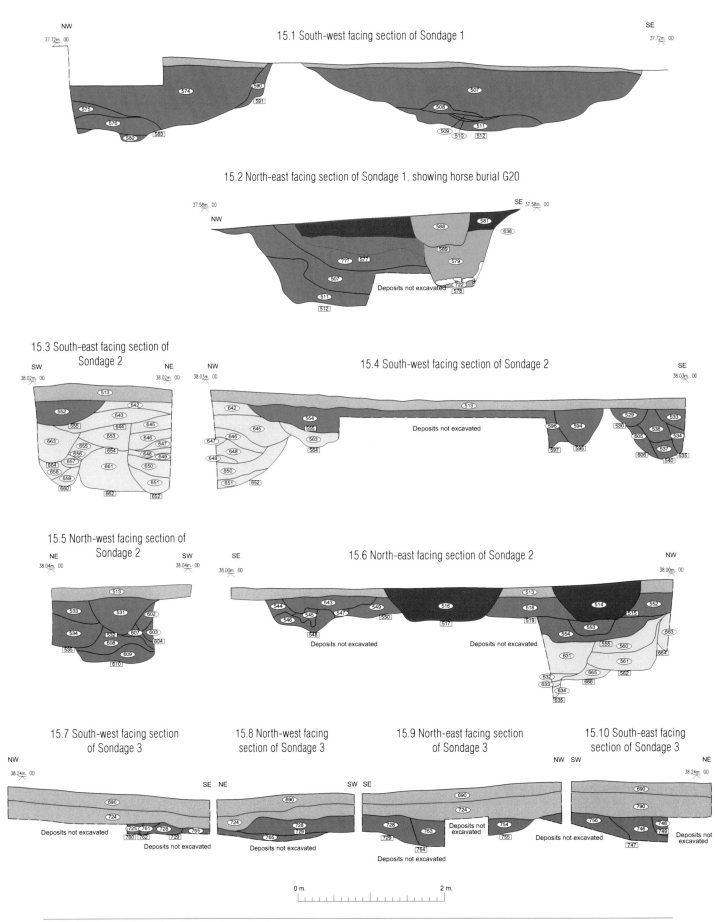

Fig 15. Sondages 1–3, sections through pit complex 2.

14

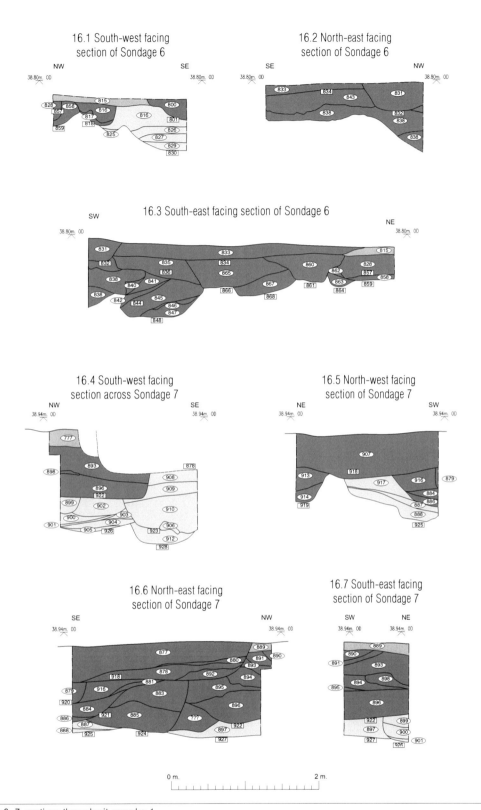

Fig 16. Sondages 6–7, sections through pit complex 1.

15

Fig 17. Early to middle Iron Age features and deposits.

2
The Excavation

Prehistoric occupation

Early prehistoric activity

Evidence of earlier prehistoric activity in the area is limited to the presence of several flint tools all found within later deposits (*see* pp 61–2). An early Palaeolithic flake tool was recovered from the fill of an early Romano-British ditch; a later Mesolithic or early Neolithic flake/fabricator was recovered from the surface of redeposited Romano-British material; and two later Neolithic blade cores were recovered, one from a pit of Iron Age date and the other from reworked soils over the pitting. No demonstrably early features were found, though a large, shallow amorphous scoop into natural (218) may have been much earlier than the rest of the features observed (Figs 18 and 19.3).

The late Bronze Age

No features could be securely dated to the late Bronze Age, although some of the earlier pits (G4, 5 and 8), boundary ditches (G2) and a hollow and burnt flint spread (G3) discussed below may owe their origins to this period. The primary evidence for activity in the late Bronze Age comes from the pottery, which has a small but significant element of material from the very latest Bronze Age 'decorated' phase (*see* p 43). It should be noted that this pottery was in poor condition and was often found in association with early Iron Age material, albeit very early forms. It is likely that this pottery is residual, possibly lying in open middens for some period prior to being cleared or washed into the pits or ditches from which it was recovered. The quantity of pottery of this date is sufficient to indicate occupation in the vicinity, most probably up the slope to the south of the site.

The early to middle Iron Age

Occupation in the early to middle Iron Age (possibly beginning slightly earlier, as noted above) was characterised by intensive pitting, bounded to the north by a roughly east–west aligned sequence of ditches (G2) (Fig 17). Between the pitting and the boundary ditches lay a broad linear hollow across the base of which was spread a deposit of burnt flint (G3).

The intensive pitting was divided into three regions or complexes: pit complex 1, to the west of the excavation area (G4 and G10); pit complex 2, to the east (G8 and G12); and pit complex 3, to the south (G5, G7 and G11). Separating the complexes were narrow exposures of geological material, probably derived from solifluxion. A narrow gravel track (G6) extended along the southern edge of excavation sealing early pits in pit complex 3 and in turn being cut by others. Lying over the pit complexes was an undifferentiated reworked soil (G14), cut by further pits and ditches, mostly belonging to the Romano-British period, though some could be prehistoric.

The northern boundary of occupation (G2) (Fig 18 and section Figs 10 and 19.1–19.5)

The northern boundary of visible activity was marked by a west-north-west to east-south-east sequence of ditches extending for *c* 40m from the west edge of excavation to its north-east corner, where it was removed by modern terracing. Three phases of ditch were identified, cutting Head Brickearth, in six slots excavated through the boundary.

In its earliest phase the boundary appears to have been formed by a broad shallow cut (222/230, 214, 216), 1.8–2m wide by 0.3–0.4m deep, observed extending at least 20m from the west section, but not identified further to the east.

The early ditch became silted up and new ditches (212/220 and 224) were cut on the same alignment. Ditch 212/220 was observed projecting 2.5m from the west edge of excavation before ending in a rounded terminal. Ditch 224 was observed 30m to the east in a slot cut across the alignment and was traced a further 6m east before being removed by the modern terracing. To the west of the slot the full extent of the ditch was not determined, but it could not have extended more than 14m in this direction as it was not detected in a slot across the earlier ditch at this point. The profiles and depths of the new ditches were very different from the earlier ditch. Ditch 212/220 had a V-shaped profile, 2.1m wide by 0.9m deep, and ditch 224 had an irregular bell-shaped profile, 1.8m wide at the (machined) surface decreasing to 0.75m wide at a depth of *c* 0.2m before dropping steeply to a rounded base at a depth of 0.6m. Although these later ditches cannot be directly linked stratigraphically, it is considered likely that they were broadly contemporary, forming a discontinuous boundary with a gap 17–30m wide.

G2
BOUNDARY DITCHES

G2
BOUNDARY DITCHES

DITCH
TERMINUS

N

0   10m.

Fig 18. Early to middle Iron Age occupation: G2, northern boundary of occupation.

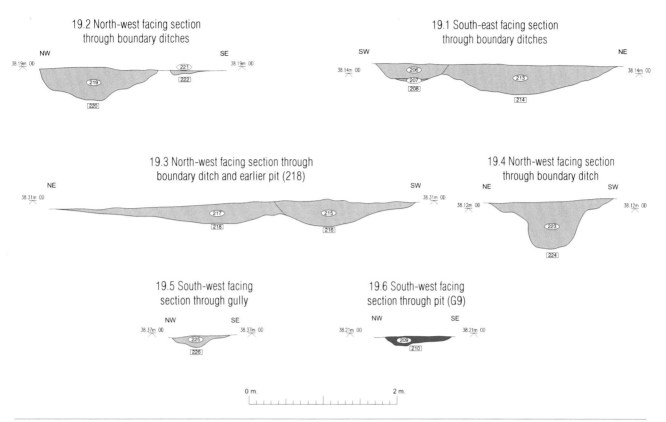

19.2 North-west facing section
through boundary ditches

19.1 South-east facing section
through boundary ditches

19.3 North-west facing section through
boundary ditch and earlier pit (218)

19.4 North-west facing section
through boundary ditch

19.5 South-west facing
section through gully

19.6 South-west facing
section through pit (G9)

0 m.   2 m.

Fig 19. Sections through prehistoric boundary ditches (G2) and pit 210 (G9).

Ditch 212/220 in turn became silted and was replaced by a narrower, shallower gully or ditch (208, 226 and 228), 0.6m wide by 0.3m deep, cutting the south side of the earlier ditches. This feature was observed for just over 18m from the west edge of excavation, becoming shallower and then disappearing, probably as a result of truncation rather than its termination.

The quantity of pottery recovered from these ditches was comparatively high and, taken together, suggests a very late Bronze Age to earliest Iron Age date for the material. However the pottery is very worn, particularly some of that in the later ditches, and is broadly contemporary across all three phases.

Bulk sampling of the fills of these ditches revealed the presence of charred cereal remains and weed seeds in their fills, most notably from ditch 224, which produced a sample of sufficient size and quality for further analysis and which indicated the presence of spelt wheat and hulled barley, along with chaff, weed seeds and also a nut (see pp 71–3). Mammal bone from cattle, goat/sheep and horse, all in poor condition, was also recovered from the fills.

Irregular linear hollow with burnt flint spread across its base (G3) (Fig 20 and sections Figs 10, 11.1, 12.1 13.1 and 13.2)

Between 1 and 5m south of the boundary lay the sinuous northern edge of a shallow hollow (305) with burnt flint spread across its base (269, 306, 426, 502 and 503). The cut for this feature was gradual, almost imperceptible in places, sloping from the north for several metres before levelling out. The hollow was traced from the west section for 45m to the modern terracing at the north-east corner of excavation. Its southern edge could not be determined with certainty, as it had been cut away by Romano-British ditches and by a modern linear intrusion truncating the sequence, but the spread of burnt flint suggests it to have been up to 20m wide.

Three small pits and a gully (282, 284, 526 and 521) were observed cutting natural geology in the base of the hollow. The relationship of these features with the hollow is unclear and it cannot be determined whether they were truncated by it or whether they were cut within it. The function of the pits was not determined and the full extent of the gully not observed, though it was broadly parallel with the northern boundary. All four were sealed by the burnt flint spread.

The burnt flint spread lying across the base of the hollow varied in thickness and flint concentration. Against the north edge of the hollow the flint was at its thickest and most concentrated, particularly close to the west edge of excavation where it was 0.3m thick; to the south it became thinner, reducing to a single flint thickness with flints becoming increasingly sporadic. Towards the centre and east of the excavation the thickness of the deposit was generally not more than 0.1m at the north, rapidly becoming untraceable to the south. The flint was mainly small to medium sized and very calcined, suggesting fairly intense firing. The burnt flint lay in a silty matrix indistinguishable

G3 EDGE OF LINEAR HOLLOW

G3 BURNT FLINT SPREAD

G3 EDGE OF LINEAR HOLLOW

G3 EDGE OF LINEAR HOLLOW

G3 BURNT FLINT SPREAD

521

493

284

282

N

0   10m.

Fig 20. Early to middle Iron Age occupation: G3 burnt flint spread within linear hollow, earlier pits and gully.

Plate 3. Late Bronze Age boundary ditch (G2) under excavation.

from the Romano-British horizons lying above it and, in places, from silts lying below the flint, the latter indicating that the flint was not a primary deposit within the hollow.

Small quantities of late Bronze Age and earliest Iron Age pottery were recovered from the pits sealed beneath the burnt flint and a sizable assemblage (135 sherds) was recovered from the burnt flint in the north-west corner of the site (269). The latter assemblage included later early Iron Age forms, dated to around 500–350 BC. Elsewhere the deposit yielded little datable material. Sampling of the earlier features produced small quantities of large mammal bone, traces of charcoal, charred grain, chaff and seeds, but the possibility of contamination from Romano-British deposits lying above is strong.

Pit complexes 1– 3: introduction (Fig 21)

The profiles, plans and dimensions of the pits forming the pit complexes were varied and it is not intended to describe them individually, unless there is specific reason. The pits ranged in size from *c* 0.3–4.5m in plan and from 0.1–1.3m in depth. Plans varied from subcircular to subrectangular, while some were amorphous. Profiles varied from U-shape to V-shape, with others less regular. Few of the pits contained more than one or two identifiable fills and most were filled by clay silts or silt clays, similar to the reworked soil (G14) above and to colluvial deposits seen elsewhere. Others contained redeposited solifluxion deposits. Finds were limited, with few pits producing ceramics and very few producing sizable

assemblages. Similarly, quantities of mammal bone were small, and where present, poorly preserved; environmental evidence was also limited and was prone to contamination from later phases. None of the pits produced sufficient quantities of charred plant remains for further analysis.

Pit complex 1 (G4 and G10) (sections Figs 11.1–11.3, 13.3 and 16.1–16.6)

Pit complex 1 lay to the west of the excavation area, covering an area *c* 10m north–south by 12–16m east–west. Only the north edge of the complex was well defined. To the south and west pitting became less intense but hard to define in the solifluxion deposits at this edge of site; to the east reworked soils made definition of its limits difficult and to the south-east the complex merged with pit complex 3.

Fifty-three pits were identified mostly beneath the reworked soil in four interventions into the complex (Trench 16 and Sondages 5–7). In all four archaeological features were excavated to the base of the sequence of intercutting pits, the deepest of which exceeded 1.2m in depth. Very few pits produced any ceramic evidence and most of those that did yielded very few sherds. Only a few pits (801, 834, 836, 848/849/851/852, 915 and 918) yielded assemblages of over forty sherds. Of the remainder only two produced more than ten sherds. Bulk sampling of several pits produced similarly limited results. Few, poorly preserved mammal bones were present along with traces of charcoal, charred grain and chaff. A few pits also yielded traces of hammerscale and yellow grey and whitish clinker suggesting waste from metalworking.

Of note within this complex was a pit (328) containing a single fragment of human skull. The skull was from an adult, of indeterminate age and sex. The pit was subrectangular to oval in plan measuring 1.7 by 1.2m with steep sides turning to a concave base at a depth of 0.6m. The skull fragment lay close to the base of the pit, *c* 150mm above it a similarly sized body sherd of a rusticated early Iron Age ceramic vessel was recovered and a further *c* 150mm above this lay a sheep/goat scapula. The type of artefacts and their arrangement within the pit is suggestive of intentional placement, indicating a 'ritual' element at least to the abandonment of the pit. However, the pottery was fairly worn and was similar to other pottery recovered from pits within the complex in which there is nothing to suggest a ritual nature and, though this does not preclude 'ritual' deposition, the evidence is limited. The silty clay fill also contained a small quantity of burnt flint and soil sampling produced fragments of mammal bone and bird bone, along with a very small quantity of charred plant remains, including chaff and weed seeds.

Four pit cuts (848/849/851/852) identified in plan after excavation were probably open simultaneously, as they were largely filled by a single sequence of deposits. Two of the fills, 845 and 850, yielded eighty-seven and thirty-seven sherds of pottery respectively, the latter also producing a fragment of a fired clay loomweight and the former a burnt clay fragment that could also have been from a weight.

PIT COMPLEX 2
(G8 AND G12)

PIT COMPLEX 3
(G5, G7 AND G11)

PIT COMPLEX 3
(G5, G7 AND G11)

PIT COMPLEX 1
(G4 AND G10)

N

0   10m.

Fig 21. Early to middle Iron Age occupation: pit complexes 1–3 (G4, G5, G7, G8, G10, G11 and G12).

Several large fragments of yellow-grey and whitish clinker or slag were recovered from the lower fill (850). It was noted (*see* p 54) that although the deposits produced joining sherds, there was wear suggesting the pottery had been exposed for some time prior to being cleared into these cuts.

A shallow pit (836) recorded as truncating the group of four pits, discussed above, yielded a further sixty-five sherds of Iron Age pottery along with a La Tène I brooch, dated to the fourth to third century BC (*see* p 63). Given the difficulties of identification of individual pits during excavation, it is considered possible that this feature was misunderstood and was not a separate feature but the upper fill of this earlier group of cuts. Another pit (914) within the complex may also relate directly to this group. The pit yielded forty-one sherds of pottery along with similar lumps of clinker or slag to those retrieved from fill 850. It is likely that this was part of the same group of open pits, filled at the same time and by the same material.

Three pits (801, 834 and 918) are included in this complex despite being identified cutting the undifferentiated reworked soil, G14, overlying it. They are included here because of the significant size of the Iron Age pottery assemblage derived from their fills and also because 834 and 918 lay over the pits discussed above. Pits 834 and 918 were probably part of a single large, irregular shaped hollow, not more than 0.4m deep, lying over the earlier pits, and again may have been contemporary. These pits had fills significantly darker than the surrounding material and yielded respectively sixty-five, forty-six and eighty-six sherds of pottery. Pit 801 also produced evidence of primary flint knapping activity.

Pit complex 2 (G8 and G12) (sections Figs 12.1, 12.2, 13.1, 13.2, 15.1–15.10)

Pit complex 2 lay to the east of the excavation area and was the most clearly defined of the three complexes. The complex measured approximately 15 by 25m at its maximum extent and was separated from those to the south and west by an outcrop of natural gravel 1.5–4m wide.

The complex was investigated in seven interventions (Trenches 17, 18, 20 and Sondages 1–4) and only locally was the sequence completely excavated to expose natural geology, at a depth of up to 1.2m. A total of sixty-six pits was identified during excavation. As with pit complex 1 few of the pits yielded any pottery and most that did produced less than ten sherds. Only six yielded more than twenty-five sherds and only four others yielded over ten. Soil sampling again produced only small quantities of material. Mammal bone was recovered in small amounts and was mostly poorly preserved. A few samples produced small quantities of charred cereal grain, chaff and other seeds, along with pea-sized pulses. However, none of the samples produced charred plant remains of sufficient size or quality to merit further analysis.

Some differences were noted in the morphology and intensity of pitting within this complex. To the west the pits were typically less than 1m in diameter and ranged from 0.3–1m in depth. The fills of these pits were slightly more numerous and varied than those in pit complex 1. Redeposited clay, flint and chalk presumably derived from excavation of solifluxion deposits in the vicinity, was mixed

Plate 4. Excavation of slots through pit complex 2 (G8 and G12).

23

Fig 22. Early to middle Iron Age occupation: trackway (G6).

with a generally darker clay-silt than that observed in the western complex. To the east the pits were larger and their cutting was less frequent, though this is possibly because these large pits belong to a very late phase of activity which has removed any evidence for intensity and size of earlier pitting. The largest of the pits observed in this complex was located on its east edge. The pit (512) was over 4.5m across in section and more than 1.2m deep, exposing solifluxion deposits of gravel in its sides and base. The lower fills yielded little other than friable fragments of mammal bone, but the upper fill (507), which filled most of its profile, produced eighty-two sherds of Iron Age pottery from a large volume of soil.

An irregular pit or cut (555), over 2m across and 0.6m deep yielded seventy-seven sherds of Iron Age pottery from its fills, along with what had probably been the complete skeleton of a neonatal calf. Although not in an identifiable cut within the pit, the deposit containing the calf skeleton was distinct from the surrounding material, being much darker and containing carbonised material. It is tempting to see this as a 'ritual' deposit, but there is no need for it to be anything other than disposal of an aborted foetus (*see* p 71). A human tooth was also recovered from sampling but otherwise no organic remains were present.

Pit complex 3 (G5) (sections Figs 12.1, 14.1 and 14.2)

Pit complex 3 lay against the central southern edge of excavation and extended to the south of the site. Its north edge lay between 3 and 5m from the edge of excavation and its east–west dimension was 16m. To the north-west the complex merged with reworked soils joining it to pit complex 1.

The pitting was only partially excavated in Trench 19 as it lay outside the reduced area of sampling. A total of eleven pits were identified pre-dating the trackway (G6). Only two of these were excavated, producing a small quantity of early Iron Age pottery.

Trackway, gully and associated pits (G6, G7 and G11) (Fig 22 and sections Figs 12.1, 14.1 and 14.2)

A thin horizon of small flint pebbles (363) within a slight hollow (447) was observed extending from the south-east corner of excavation clipping the south edge of pit complex 1 and extending across the north edge of pit complex 3, curving gradually for 30m to head under the south edge of excavation (G6). The hollow was between 1 and 2m wide and was not more than 0.15m deep. The flint horizon was 30mm thick at maximum and was loosely formed. The only obvious function for this feature was as a trackway, though the metalling was basic and would not have taken much wear. Bulk sampling of the trackway produced small burnt flint fragments, charred cereal grain and chaff, along with fragmentary large mammal bone and whelk. The plant material was considered of sufficient quantity and quality to merit detailed analysis. As with the material derived from

ditch 224 (G2) spelt wheat and barley were identified, along with chaff and glume bases, indicating processing of cereal crops (*see* pp 71–3) However this material could all have derived from overlying Romano-British deposits in close contact, which contained similar material, and so its presence is of limited significance to the prehistoric period.

A short stretch of U-shaped gully (275 (G6)), 0.5m wide and 0.2m deep, was observed 0.5m to the north of the trackway at the west edge of excavation. The gully appeared to run parallel to the trackway for 7m before being lost in disturbance around pit complexes 1 and 3. No cultural material was retrieved from this feature but spatially it seems likely to be associated with the track.

How long the track remained in use is unclear, but eight pits (G7) were observed cutting into it in Trench 19, although most of these only clipped it. Only four of these pits were excavated. The excavated pits varied in form and size, the smallest being subcircular, measuring 0.5m in diameter and only 0.1m in depth and the largest subrectangular, measuring 1.2 by 1.4m by 0.6m deep. The latter pit (377) was identified in the field as being used as a rubbish pit with 'occupation' material within its fills. However, pottery (dating to the early to middle Iron Age) was only recovered from the upper fill along with a small quantity of large mammal bone. Bulk sampling of all its fills indicated small quantities of charred cereal grain and chaff, the latter more prominent in the upper fill, but little else to support this interpretation. The quantity of cereal grain was not sufficient to justify further analysis.

A thin lens of clay silt (362 (G11)) formed over the track and sealed much of the subsequent pitting, though two pits (375, 421 (G11)) clearly post-dated it. The latter yielded a small quantity of early to middle Iron Age pottery. Whether the silt represented abandonment of the track or not is uncertain. The two pits had cut sufficiently into the track to suggest that it was no longer in use by the time they were cut, but their dating is uncertain and the prehistoric pottery recovered from pit 421 may be residual within a Roman pit and so it is possible that the track remained in use till the end of the early Iron Age occupation.

Pits to the north of the prehistoric boundary (G9) (Fig 23 and section Fig 19.6)

A small cluster of pits (203, 205, 210) was observed immediately to the north of the prehistoric boundary (G2), in the north-west corner of the site. These were shallow, no more than 0.3m deep, and two (203, 205) appear to be the truncated remnant of rubbish pits: animal bone, a quern/ rubbing stone fragment, from 203, and domestic pottery were recovered from their fills. They were subcircular in plan, measuring respectively 1.3 and 1.6m in diameter. The third was less regular and did not contain domestic waste. Bulk sampling of pit 203 produced traces of ?bronzeworking slag and hammerscale along with small quantities of large and small mammal, bird, amphibian and fish bones. Perhaps significant in the light of the presence of the possible

G9
?RUBBISH
PITS

210

205

203

G13
FEATURES ON
WEST EDGE OF
PIT COMPLEX

293
295

357

369

384.5

N

0   10m.

Fig 23. Early to middle Iron Age occupation: pits (G9) north of northern boundary G2 and pits (G13) west of pit complex 1.

quern/rubbing stone was the recovery of small amounts of charcoal, charred grain, chaff and seed, indicative of cereal processing. Though, as with the neighbouring ditches, it must be considered that this may be contamination from Romano-British deposits lying directly above.

The pottery from the two rubbish pits was of late Bronze Age and early Iron Age date, but was quite abraded. It is suggested by McNee (p 54) that the wear is consistent with the pottery having been exposed in a rubbish dump which was subsequently cleared into these pits.

Possible cremation or votive vessel north of the prehistoric boundary (G9)

Only one other feature was identified north of the boundary ditch. A suspected cremation vessel (570) was located during a watching brief on building works (plot 33) 15m east of the site and 10m north of the projected line of the boundary. The vessel was truncated by machine, but was clearly associated with an area of redeposited burnt material. However no calcined bone was recovered in association with the pot. The cut in which this deposit sat was poorly defined as a result of machine damage and cannot be described.

The vessel was a rusticated form of early Iron Age date and appears to have been broken a short time before deposition (see p 54). Bulk sampling produced no bone of any sort, but did produce charcoal and a few seeds from around the vessel. These were insufficient in quantity or quality to merit further analysis. Whether the deposits represented burial or votive deposition following ritual breaking of the pot, or were simply rubbish, could not be determined. The absence of bone, if this was a cremation, could be for several reasons: it may have never been included either intentionally or accidentally or it could have been lost through post-depositional activity, eg through truncation by machine.

Pits lying to the west of pit complex 1 (G13) (Fig 23)

A small group of five intercutting pits (295, 357, 358, 369 and 384/385) was observed in Trench 15 immediately west of pit complex 1. Only one of the pits (369) produced cultural material, four sherds of Iron Age pottery and four of early Roman pottery, the latter thought to be intrusive. The functions of these pits were not determined.

Reworked soils over pit complexes (G14) (Fig 24 and sections Figs 10, 11.1, 12.2, 13.3, 14.1, 14.2 15.1, 15.3– 15.10, 16.1, 16.3, 16.4, 16.6 and 16.7)

The three pit complexes, the metalled trackway and, to some extent, the burnt flint spread were masked by a homogeneous clay silt horizon, distinguished from the Romano-British soil horizon above by the presence of identifiable pits cutting its surface. The origin of this soil is uncertain, but it is probable that it resulted from a combination of factors. The extent of the

pitting suggests that the contemporary ground surface would have been very disturbed, both from excavation and from movement of people and animals. Other activities conducted in the area may also have contributed. This reworking of the area will have resulted in the homogenisation of the upper pit fills and the creation of hollows and depressions in its surface. These hollows and depressions, along with open pits are likely to have held water and to have made the area seasonally boggy, further homogenising the soils. Wind- and water-borne erosion deposits along with vegetation and faunal activity will have contributed to this process. That the soil was susceptible to becoming boggy is supported by the observation of limescale on the surface of pottery from the deposit, which is indicative of the pottery having lain in waterlogged ground (see p 54).

The small quantity of pottery recovered from the deposit included both Iron Age and Romano-British material. Only in one intervention was a significant quantity of pottery recovered from the deposit (724, Sondage 3), dating to the early to middle Iron Age, though this may have come from the upper fill of a pit. Of note was the presence of seven fresh flakes of struck flint in the upper spit of soil (690) removed from the same intervention. These are suggested to be debitage from a primary episode of flint knapping and therefore in situ (see p 61).

Formation of the soil probably took place over a substantial period of time, beginning in the Iron Age and continuing into the early Roman period, when further pitting took place. However the presence of primary flint knapping material suggests that the process of formation was largely complete by the end of the Iron Age. The presence of Romano-British pottery beneath the soil horizon indicates that some pits had either not been identified properly and their correct stratigraphic position not determined or that the process of homogenisation was ongoing into the Roman period, or both.

Discussion

The excavation is thought to have located the northern periphery of a larger site lying to the south of the development area, further up the slope. Pit complex 3, the metalled trackway and a scatter of isolated pits were all observed extending beneath the south edge of excavation. To the west it is clear that occupation extended towards the garden of No 246 Dover Road (the A258) as the northern boundary ditches, the hollow and burnt flint spread all extended in this direction, along with several pits. To the east the limit of occupation was less well defined. The ditches had been removed by modern terracing, along with the burnt flint spread, which was in any case becoming less evident. The depth of overburden and the increasing uniformity of deposits in this direction further made definition difficult. The subsequent watching brief suggested pitting to have continued east for at least another 15m, but beyond this it was not identified. To the north and further east, evaluation and watching brief produced very little evidence for activity,

27

Fig 24. Iron Age and early Romano-British reworked soil G14 masking pit complexes 1–3.

0   10m.

N

with the exception of the possible cremation or votive deposit found under plot 33 (Fig 7).

Because of the limited area of the site exposed it is not possible to discuss at any length the nature, form or chronology of the occupation. Although no evidence for structures was identified the quantity of domestic material, ceramic and faunal, does indicate the proximity of habitation. The observation of boundary ditches suggests that this settlement was at least partially enclosed in its earliest phases, but by the end of the early Iron Age the situation is less clear although the boundary appears to have remained in some form.

Occupation of the site began towards the end of the later Bronze Age, though no features can be securely dated to this period. It is likely that the boundary ditches were dug at a fairly early stage of this occupation and that they had a relatively long life span. The worn state of the pottery and the consistency of its date in the infill of all three phases of ditch suggests that the pottery was lying exposed for some time prior to entering ditches and that it was derived from the same source, presumably open middens close to the boundary, most probably on its north side given the site topography. No pottery, fresh or worn, of later early to middle Iron Age date was recovered, suggesting that the ditches had ceased to exist as a prominent feature by this time. However, the longevity of the boundary is supported by the relative absence of identifiable activity to its north and its presence may have been marked by fences or hedges in the later phases of occupation.

It is difficult to determine the scale and nature of the boundary represented by the ditches: their depth and form varied between the three phases and they had probably been significantly truncated. No traces of an internal bank, palisade or other structures were identifiable and the position of the hollow and burnt flint spread, if contemporary, suggest that these were unlikely to have existed. The discontinuous nature of the ditches may indicate an entrance to the site, but the extensive pitting to its south suggests that either this was no longer in existence by the time this was occurring, or that the boundary had taken a different form along this short stretch, such as a fence or hedge. The only excavated ditch terminal produced no evidence for placed or special deposits, seen in ditch terminals at many sites.

The nature of the hollow in which burnt flint was deposited is ambiguous and its origin, whether natural or man-made, not determined. The position of the hollow on the north edge of a possible natural hollow or valley head may be of relevance. It is possible that it was formed by wear along the edge of this feature and/or intentional removal of deposits from its side to form a terrace. The burnt flint lying across its base did not appear primary and was not consistent or compact enough to have formed a metalled surface. It is therefore unlikely to have been a track or yard area. The source of the flint is unclear; there was no trace of *in situ* burning, but the volume of flint suggests it to be locally derived. The distribution of flint suggests tipping into the hollow from its north, particularly to the west, indicating

that it may have originated from unknown activity west or north-west of the excavation area. Whether the flint can be considered to form a 'burnt mound', or to be derived from one, is uncertain and the function of such features is in any case ambiguous. The relationship between the hollow and boundary suggests that the two were contemporary, as the line of the hollow seems to broadly follow that of the ditches. However the pottery recovered from the burnt flint indicates that its deposition was later than the material infilling the ditches, though the latter was not primary deposition.

The primary activity represented in this area of the site seems to have been the excavation of pits, initially perhaps for quarrying brickearth and possibly gravels. The positioning of the pitting within the suspected natural hollow or valley head is possibly no coincidence, as a variety of solifluxion deposits were present including both these resources. However the reasons for continued pitting, recutting earlier fills, are unclear. It is also interesting to note that the boundary ditches were located on the north shoulder of the hollow or valley head, rather than on the uphill side, closer to the presumed occupation. This may suggest that whatever the function, or functions, of the area it was sufficiently important to be included within the settlement. The concentration of pits may also indicate zoning of activities, but in the absence of better understanding of the activity or activities represented or of the layout of the remainder of the site, this is speculative.

The pitting is difficult to interpret and phase. Generally the stratigraphically earlier pits were aceramic and where pottery was present it was small, well worn and low in quantity. The ceramics from these earlier pits tended to belong to the very late Bronze Age or earliest Iron Age. Later deposits, though still largely aceramic, tended to have more early to middle Iron Age pottery, again showing a lot of wear. From this it is argued that the pitting took place over a considerable period, probably lasting the better part of the life of the site.

From the variation in size and form it is clear that the range of functions represented by the pits was wide. None of the features showed structural elements or traces of clay lining and the plans and profiles do not on the whole appear to fall into the types suggested for storage, perhaps most extensively studied at Danebury (Cunliffe 1991a, 153–63) and identified at many other sites of this period. The state of the pottery from the overlying reworked soil suggests that it had lain in waterlogged or boggy ground, and this suggests the area may have been unsuitable for storage. The low quantity of domestic waste recovered does not support rubbish disposal as a primary function and the limited cultural evidence retrieved adds little to their interpretation. Similarly the environmental evidence is not of sufficient quality to contribute meaningfully to the interpretation. A number of the pits had been cut where soliflucted brickearth was present and these may have been quarrying this resource for daub for building or for pottery manufacture, though there is no direct evidence for either on site. The later pits, however, cannot have been intended for this purpose as they cut into the backfill of earlier pits.

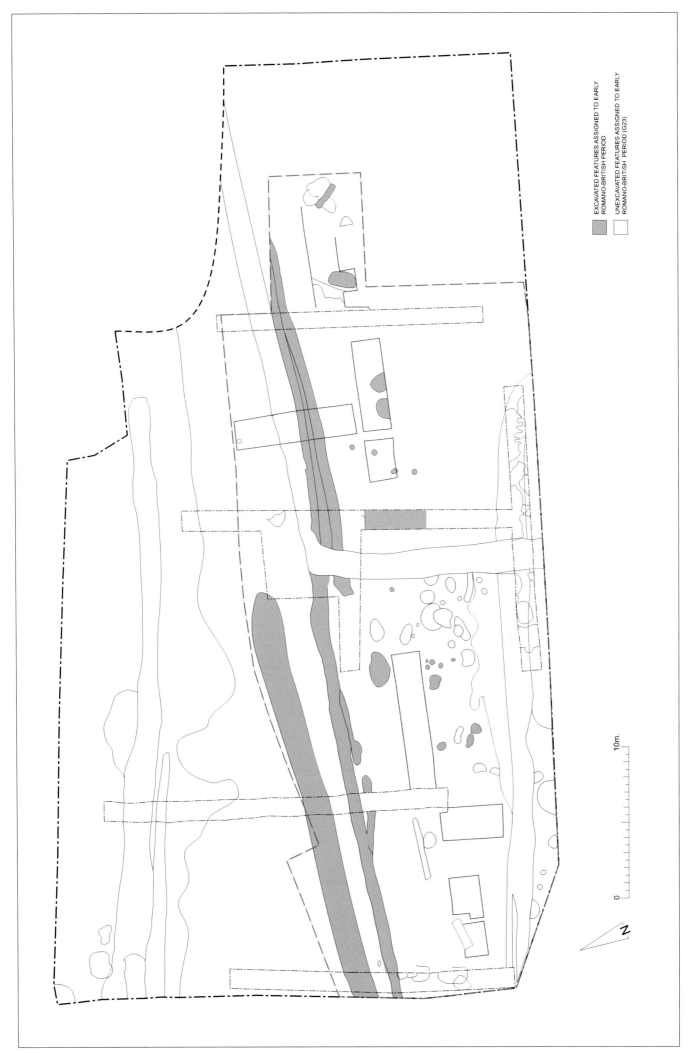

EXCAVATED FEATURES ASSIGNED TO EARLY
ROMANO-BRITISH PERIOD

UNEXCAVATED FEATURES ASSIGNED TO EARLY
ROMANO-BRITISH PERIOD (G23)

N

0   10m.

Fig 25. Early Romano-British features.

Fig 26. Early Romano-British occupation: boundary ditches (G15 and G16) and gullies (G17).

G18 MODIFIED
BOUNDARY DITCH

G18 MODIFIED
BOUNDARY DITCH

497

408

706

252

702

292

10m.

0

N

Fig 27. Early Romano-British occupation: modified boundary ditch (G18).

Only around twelve of the pits yielded more than twenty-five sherds of pottery and of those that did most were late in the sequence and several were clearly related. Conjoining sherds were present in some of the fills of the later pits and it is conjectured that some were open simultaneously. The wear patterns on the pottery suggest that this was not primary deposition and that the pottery had been cleared from rubbish deposits elsewhere on the site into these pits, perhaps in one event. Of note is the association of a La Tène I brooch, within pit 836, with one of the larger assemblages of pottery (sixty-five sherds).

The presence of a neonatal calf skeleton (pit 555), the suspected cremation or votive vessel (570), the fragment of human skull (pit 328) and a second fragment found in a Roman pit (476, below) may indicate 'ritual' deposition. The disproportionate presence of human skull fragments at various sites has been noted, eg All Cannings Cross, Wiltshire, and it is suggested that skulls were subject to special treatment with fragments retained as tokens (Cunliffe 1991b, 506–7). The apparent placement of the skull fragment in pit 328, with a similarly sized slightly worn pottery sherd and sheep scapula above, each separated by around 150mm of infill, is strongly suggestive of 'ritual' action. The second skull fragment, though found in a pit dated to the early Roman phase, may come from a similar deposit. Notably, with the exception of a probable early Roman inhumation, the only other human remains recovered from the site was a single tooth, associated with the neonatal calf. As noted the neonatal calf may be simple rubbish disposal, but analysis at Danebury has suggested a 'ritual' pattern of deposition of complete or partial animal, human and artefactual material (Cunliffe 1995, 80–8). Both the calf burial and the broken pot could represent such votive deposition and the suspicion that the vessel had been broken some time before deposition tends to reinforce this suggestion over cremation burial. It should also be noted that the burial of a horse, assigned to the early Roman period (*see* pp 34–5), could belong to the early to middle Iron Age and could also be of a 'ritual' nature.

Romano-British occupation

Early Romano-British occupation

The pottery record indicates that the site was reoccupied in the early Roman period, possibly close to the Roman conquest and there was no evidence for late Iron Age pottery types to indicate earlier settlement. The principal feature of the early Roman period was a series of ditches (G15, G16 and G18) forming the north boundary of occupation (Fig 25). In its earliest phase this boundary was formed by two ditches: the eastern boundary ditch (G15) and the western boundary ditch (G16), separated by a causeway. To the south of the boundary a number of pits (G21) cut the Iron Age reworked soil G14, most of these probably dating to the Roman period. Some of the pits within the prehistoric complexes discussed above may also have been of this date. The burials of a child

(G19) and of a horse (G20) are thought to date to this period, though either could be earlier. No features of Roman date were identified to the north of the boundary ditches.

Early Romano-British boundary ditches (G15 and G16) (Fig 26 and sections Figs 10, 11.1, 12.1, 12.2, 13.1 and 13.2)

The eastern boundary ditch, G15 (402, 459, 501 and 686), was aligned south-east to north-west, extending *c* 24m from the east edge of excavation before ending in a slightly squared terminus. The ditch had a U-shaped profile, 0.75m wide by 0.4m deep to the east, increasing to 1.2m wide by 0.6m deep to the west. The ditch had undergone at least one phase of recutting (456, 499) and had been largely truncated by later modification and by the cutting of a later Romano-British ditch (G27). The only cultural materials retrieved from its fills were five sherds of Iron Age pottery, which were likely to be derived from earlier pits through which the ditch was cut.

Approximately 6m to the north of the terminal end of the eastern boundary ditch was the west terminus of the western boundary ditch G16 (290, 256). Aligned north-west to south-east, the ditch was traced for 28m from its rounded terminus to the west limit of excavation, on a parallel axis to that of the eastern boundary ditch. The terminal end of the ditch was not excavated. The ditch had a U-shape profile and was about 1.2 m wide. The full depth was not observed as a result of truncation by a linear modern feature, but it had been over 0.6m deep. The ditch appeared to have been recut on at least one occasion (254, 288), though evidence suggests a second phase of recutting was missed. The ditch produced a small quantity of late first- to second-century pottery and also the skeleton of an adult dog. The dog showed evidence of having been skinned prior to burial, a not uncommon Roman practice. Whether this represents ritual activity or simple disposal is open to discussion and, as Bendrey points out (p 71), the two may not be mutually exclusive. Bulk sampling also produced a small quantity of charred grain and chaff of insufficient quantity or quality to merit further analysis.

The relationship between the eastern and western boundary ditches could not be demonstrated stratigraphically and is based on their spatial association. The arrangement of these ditches suggests a dog-legged boundary with a causeway at the dog-leg forming a 6m wide, east facing entrance to the settlement. No pits were identified to suggest associated entry structures.

Gullies predating modification of the boundary ditch (G17) (Fig 26 and section Fig 28.1)

Three sections of curving U-shaped gully (704, 708 and 719), *c* 0.5m wide by 0.2m deep, were observed predating a modification of the early Romano-British boundary. Two sections, 704 and 708 probably formed a single length separated from the third, 719, by a *c* 1m wide causeway.

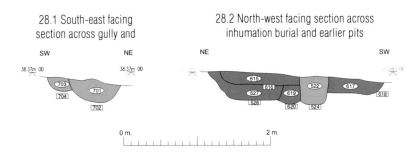

Fig 28. Section through Romano-British gully (G17), modified boundary ditch (G18) and cut of inhumation burial (G19).

Gully 704/708 was observed for 7m and 719 for 8m. The gullies were cut away to the north by the later boundary ditch (G18) and their respective eastern and western extents had been lost. The date of these gullies is unclear, though early Roman pottery was recovered from one and they were identified cutting the reworked soil, G14. The function of these gullies and relationship with the earlier boundary ditches and other features could not be determined.

Modification to Romano-British boundary (G18) (Fig 27 and sections Figs 10, 11.1, 12.1, 12.2, 13.1, 13.2 and 28.1)

The early Romano-British boundary was modified, probably in the second century, by the cutting of a single ditch (252, 292, 408, 497, 702 and 706) along the line of the earlier, eastern boundary ditch, G15, extending on the

Plate 5. Inhumation burial of a child (G19) under excavation.

same alignment to meet the west edge of excavation. The ditch had a U-shape profile: to the east it was 0.9m wide by 0.5m deep, while to the west it had been largely truncated by a linear modern feature. Bulk sampling from the ditch produced small quantities of charred cereal remains and chaff, again of insufficient quantity for detailed analysis. The small quantity of pottery recovered from the fills was dated to the late first or second century.

Inhumation burial (G19) (Fig 29 and section Fig 28.2)

The inhumation burial of a child was located towards the east limit of the excavation, less than 5m south of the Romano-British boundary ditches. The body had been laid supine within a shallow rectangular cut (524) 1.8m long by 0.6m wide. The grave was aligned slightly north of north-west to south-east with the head to the south. The skeleton (523) was reasonably well preserved. The presence of unerupted teeth and the general appearance of the skeleton indicate that it was that of a juvenile, perhaps ten to thirteen years old. Pathology was limited, but there were indications of malnutrition or childhood disease in the tooth development and of anaemia in the bone record. A full assessment of the skeleton is held in the site archive.

The burial was not accompanied by any grave goods and no incidental finds were found within its backfill. Bulk sampling failed to produce any artefactual or environmental material. The burial was assigned to this period in part because of the relatively good condition of the bone and the form of the interment, though it is possible that it is earlier and stratigraphically it could only be demonstrated to predate the middle Roman period.

Horse burial (G20) (Fig 29 and section Fig 15.2)

Approximately 5m to the west of the child's grave was the burial of a horse, cut into the eastern edge of prehistoric pit complex 2. The pit (578) in which it had been interred was oval, measuring 2 by 1.5m and was less than 1m deep. The animal, though relatively small, had been squeezed into the pit: its legs were broken and folded up against the west edge, and its head tucked in against its chest. The cut was aligned north-west to south-east with the head to the north.

The skeleton (722) was in reasonable condition, except for the skull, which was removed prior to the recognition of

Plate 6. Horse skeleton (G20). The skull was removed in an earlier intervention. Scale 1m.

remainder of the body, and which fell apart on excavation. Study of the skeleton (*see* pp 68–70) has indicated interesting pathology, suggesting the horse was diseased, suffering from either tuberculosis or brucellosis. However, this was not necessarily the cause of death, at least not directly. The age of the horse has been estimated at 7–10 years and there are no signs of butchery on the carcass, except for the breaking of limbs, which probably occurred immediately prior to burial. Whether the burial represents disposal of a diseased animal or ritual deposition is unclear and as Bendrey points out (pp 70–1) the two are not necessarily exclusive in earlier societies.

Features cutting reworked soil (G21 and G23) (Fig 29 and sections Figs 12.1 and 15.6)

Twenty-five pits were investigated cutting into the reworked soil horizon (G14) masking the earlier pit complexes. Approximately twenty further features were planned but not investigated as they lay within the back gardens of the proposed houses, outside the reduced area of sample excavation. These features varied in size and form. Functions could not generally be determined, although around half were of a suitable size to suggest that they were post-holes.

Only one group of four small post-holes (483, 485, 489 and 491) could be suggested to be related. The post-holes were each separated by 0.8m and were arranged in two pairs, sharing the same alignment, with the northern pair offset 0.5m to the east. Whether they were associated is not clear, but they may have formed a linear arrangement with a dog-leg between the second and third post settings.

A shallow, subcircular pit (517), 1.3m in diameter by 0.3m deep, cutting the reworked soil over pit complex 2, in

Sondage 2, produced a small assemblage of early to middle Iron Age pottery along with some first-century sherds and a well preserved La Tène III style pin brooch of first-century BC or early first-century AD date (*see* p 63).

A large, partially excavated, subrectangular pit (476), with a visible dimension of 4.8m and a depth of over 0.5m, yielded forty-two sherds of early to middle Iron Age pottery along with two sherds of early first-century AD material. The dating of this feature is entirely based on the sherds of Roman pottery, which could be intrusive so the feature may be earlier. Of significance was the finding of a fragment of human skull, probably from an adult, but insufficient survived to determine age, sex or pathology. Although presumed redeposited in this pit, it is possible that it came from a similar context to a skull fragment found in one of the pits forming prehistoric pit complex 1 (328) discussed above, and may therefore represent 'ritual' deposition. The skull fragments were clearly not matching and so the two pieces do not represent a single individual.

Dating evidence from most of these features was absent or sparse. Where present it included early to middle Iron Age and early Roman pottery. The Roman pottery was generally in good condition and suggests that it had not been exposed long before burial, the prehistoric material on the other hand was much more abraded. The pits are dated to the Romano-British period largely on the basis of their being identified cutting through the reworked soil and it is possible that some of these date to the earlier period of occupation. Bulk sampling of several pits within the group produced only insignificant traces of charred plant remains. However a single post-hole (668) produced a small quantity of charred grain, chaff, a pea-sized pulse and other seeds.

Fig 29. Early Romano–British occupation: inhumation burial (G19), horse burial (G20) and pits (G21 and G23).

Middle Roman occupation

Towards the end of the second century or early in the third century AD the prehistoric and early Romano-British features were sealed beneath an undulating, heterogeneous soil horizon (G24) into which were set the foundations of a large aisled building (G26) and an associated ditch (G27). Only two other features were associated with this phase of activity.

Late second- or early third-century AD Romano-British soil horizon (G24) (Fig 30 and sections Figs 10, 11.1, 11.2, 12.1, 12.2, 14.1 and 14.2)

A heterogeneous soil horizon extended across the entire southern and central parts of the site, extending north as far as the edge of the prehistoric linear hollow (G3). The soil horizon varied in depth from around 0.2–0.6m with its upper surface undulating considerably, especially to the north and east, away from the foundations of the aisled building (G26). To the west the horizon consisted of a series of dumps of material probably derived from clearance of domestic occupation, pit digging and other activities, combined with an element of colluvial deposition. Much of the material is probably the result of secondary clearance given the state of wear and the mixture of pottery recovered. To the east the soil horizon became more uniform in its composition, with a more colluvial appearance, and by the eastern limit of excavation it had become virtually impossible to differentiate from the pit complexes it sealed and post-Roman colluvium above it.

Only a small quantity of finds was recovered from the soil horizon as hand excavation was very limited. The pottery recovered consisted of well worn first-century material and second- to early third-century material, along with well worn prehistoric ceramics. Although most of this probably derived from redeposition from elsewhere it is suggested that the soil horizon was formed in the late second or early third century, possibly as late as the mid third century. Three fragments of a quern were also recovered from the deposit.

Phasing of depositional events within this accumulated horizon is not possible, given the nature of investigation and the mixture of material within its component deposits. It is not clear whether it took place over a long period or whether it was the result of a single action of clearance from another part of the site. Similarly it is not obvious whether it was intended as a levelling deposit, filling the depressions left by pitting and levelling out of the suggested dry valley, possibly to form a platform for the construction of the aisled building.

Terracing for building construction (G25) (Fig 30 and sections Figs 11.1, 11.2, 14.1, 14.2)

During the recording of machine cut Trenches 16 and 19, through the Romano-British soil horizon G24, traces of possible terracing for the construction of an aisled building were observed. A shallow cut (301 and 390), c 0.2m deep, was identified in section and tentatively traced in plan,

extending around the building, some 4–5m from its walls. The edges of the terrace sloped gently towards the building levelling out at the same depth as its foundations. Definition of this cut was poor as the material filling it (234, 235, 236, 239, 300, 388 and 389) was virtually identical to the surrounding soil horizon, presumably because it was derived from the material which had been excavated from the soil horizon to form the terrace in the first place.

The relationship of the deposits filling the terrace with the wall foundations and post-pads of the aisled building were ambiguous, no cuts being identifiable for either. The post-holes, on the other hand clearly post-dated this material.

Pottery recovered from the deposits within the terrace was generally of late second- to mid third-century date and is virtually identical to that recovered from the surrounding soil horizon, G24. Again residual prehistoric material was present. A small quantity of late Roman and early medieval (Anglo-Saxon) pottery was recovered during surface collection from layer 239. This material was in fairly fresh condition, but its stratigraphic position makes it difficult to use in dating the deposits encountered.

Bulk sampling of deposits within the terrace, both inside and outside of the building, produced charred cereal grain, chaff, pulses and other seeds. Detailed analysis of material from deposit 235 indicated the presence of significant quantities of cereal grain and waste from processing, suggesting that processing of grain may have taken place in or around the building (*see* pp 74–5).

Aisled building (G26) (Fig 30 and sections Figs 31.1–3)

The northern 7–8m of the foundations of an aisled building lay within the excavated area, its southern end lying to the south of the excavation probably extending into adjacent field. The building was c 13m wide, aligned north-north-east to south-south-west, and was of unknown length. Within the building were two pairs of post-pads and post-holes, c 4m apart, located c 2.8m from the side walls. The aisled structure thus formed had a central hall c 6m across with aisles c 2.6m wide, allowing for its posts.

Only the lower courses of the wall foundations and aisle post settings survived. The wall foundations (231, 232, 233 and 250) were substantial, measuring c 0.8m wide, constructed from large flint nodules and rounded beach pebbles set in two interlocking courses, apparently bonded by clay. The northern pair of aisle posts appear to have sat on circular pads of flint (241 and 277), c 0.8m in diameter. The southern pair had been set in flint-packed post-holes (240 and 245). The post-holes were 0.8m in diameter with post-pipes of 0.35m diameter suggesting timbers of around this dimension. Whether these post-holes replaced earlier post-pads in order to strengthen the structure cannot be determined.

No clear cut was observed for the construction of the wall foundations, or for the post-pads, and it could be that they were constructed within the possible terracing, G25,

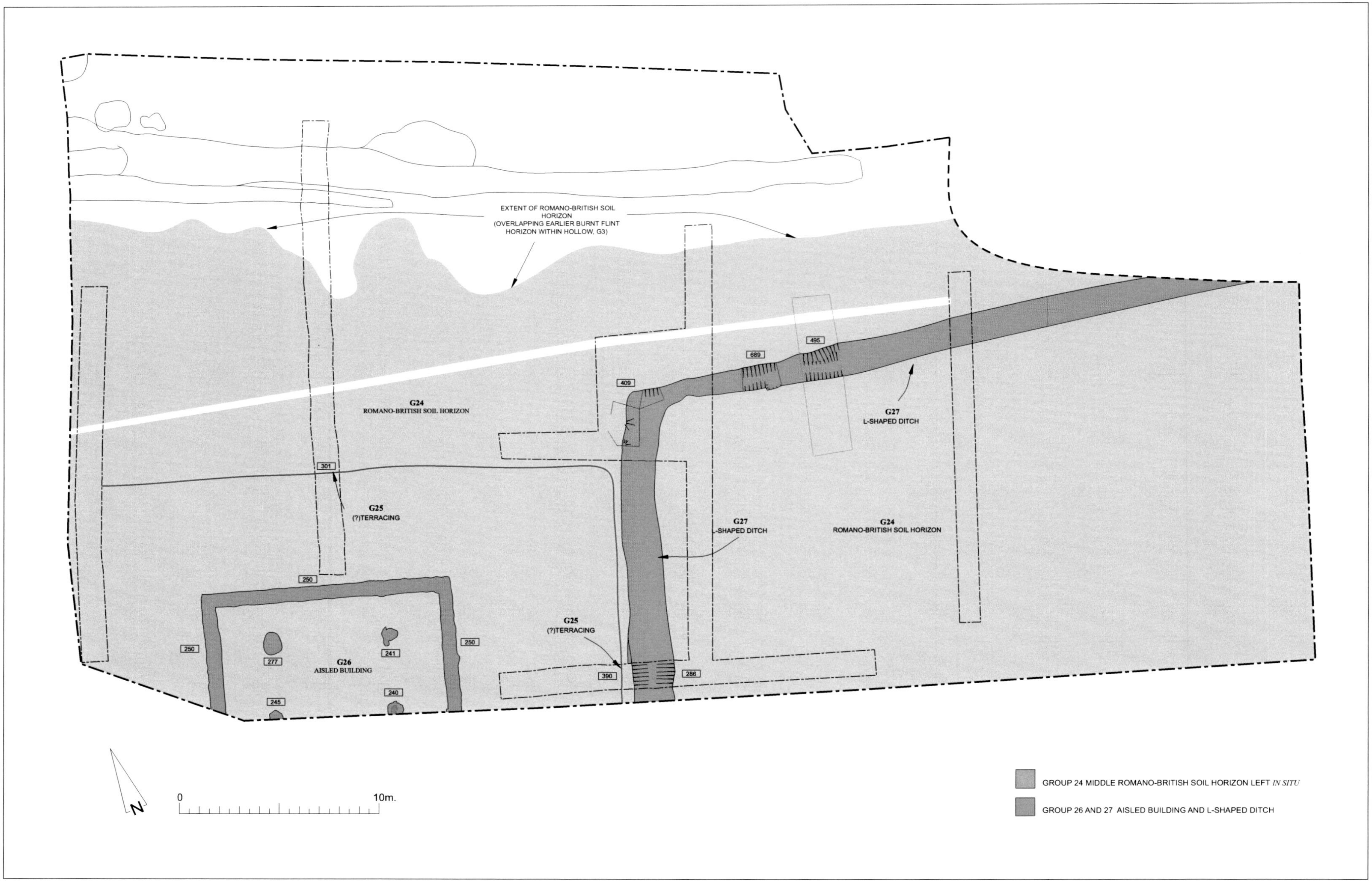

GROUP 24 MIDDLE ROMANO-BRITISH SOIL HORIZON LEFT *IN SITU*

GROUP 26 AND 27 AISLED BUILDING AND L-SHAPED DITCH

G27
L-SHAPED DITCH

G24
ROMANO-BRITISH SOIL HORIZON

495

689

G27
L-SHAPED DITCH

288

EXTENT OF ROMANO-BRITISH SOIL
HORIZON
(OVERLAPPING EARLIER BURNT FLINT
HORIZON WITHIN HOLLOW, G3)

409

390

G25
(?)TERRACING

G24
ROMANO-BRITISH SOIL HORIZON

G25
(?)TERRACING

307

290

250

241

240

G26
AISLED BUILDING

277

245

250

10m.

0

N

Fig 30. Mid Romano-British occupation: soil horizon (G24), terracing for G26 aisled building (G25) and ditch (G27).

Plate 7. Roman aisled building (G26) under excavation.

Plate 8. Roman aisled building (G26) viewed from the south-west. Scale 2m.

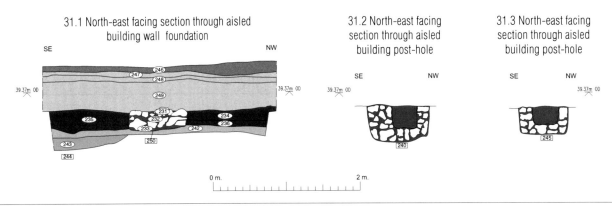

Fig 31. Section through Romano-British aisled building wall foundation and post-holes.

described above. The construction of the foundation was strong enough for it to have sat free standing with a fair weight upon it. However, the post-holes were clearly cut through the deposit filling the terrace, contradicting this idea, unless they were a later alteration.

No trace of floors or other internal features survived within the building, suggesting that there had been a phase of truncation. This is supported by the shallow depth of the foundations. The extent of truncation cannot be assessed and so the original depth of the foundations cannot be determined. It is therefore difficult to assess the load bearing capacity of the structure and thus to determine its superstructure. The presence of post-holes within the building suggests that a timber-framed structure was supported by the walls, yet the width of foundations is far greater than would seem necessary for such a building.

L-shaped ditch (G27) (Fig 30 and sections Figs 12.1, 13.1, 13.2, 14.1, 14.2)

An L-shaped ditch (286, 409, 495 and 689) lay some 8m to the east of the building, extending from the southern edge of excavation, north-north-east for a distance of *c* 15m and then turning through 90° to head east-south-east, continuing to the east limit of excavation. The ditch was up to 2.8m wide with a V-shaped profile *c* 1m deep.

The ditch turned eastward on the same alignment as the early Romano-British ditches, G15 and G18, and although they were sealed beneath the middle Roman soil horizon, G24, it is possible that the boundary they had marked remained a feature of the landscape.

The ditch was at least partially backfilled intentionally as, against the south edge of excavation, it was filled with a deposit (285) consistent with disposal of occupation material. This material was much darker than the deposits making up the surrounding soil horizon, G24, though the pottery recovered was largely of a similar date range, AD 175–200 or possibly slightly later. The deposit produced: mammal bone from cattle, pig, horse and dog; shellfish including oyster, mussel, edible winkle, limpet; and charred cereal grain and chaff. Detailed analysis of two samples from the deposit indicated the presence of both spelt wheat and barley (*see*

pp 72–3). The high quantity of chaff and the low quantity of weed seeds is suggested to indicate cereal processing. The presence of germinated wheat was noted and may be an indicator that malting was taking place, possibly for the brewing of beer. To the north and along its eastern arm the backfill of the ditch was more consistent with silting and this material produced significantly less pottery and no environmental evidence.

When the backfilling of the ditch occurred is difficult to determine given the likely secondary nature of deposition within it. Deposit 285, filling its southern extent, presumably came from surface clearance of deposits or removal of open middens, presumably relating to the use of the aisled building. However the exact relationship cannot be determined and the deposit also contained sherds of late Roman and early medieval (Anglo-Saxon) pottery, possibly indicating a later date, though these may be intrusive.

Other Romano-British features (G28) (sections Figs 11.2, 12.2)

Two pits were tentatively identified belonging to the later phase of Romano-British occupation, one in Trench 16 (303) and one in Trench 18 (411). Little can be said about these pits and no cultural material was recovered from either.

The end of the Romano-British sequence and post-Roman deposition (sections Figs 10 and 14.1)

No deposits could be identified relating to abandonment of the site and it is suspected that there had been a phase of truncation which had removed much of the evidence relating to the Romano-British building, possibly also removing any evidence for late Roman occupation.

A 0.5m deep layer of colluvial material sealed the Romano-British deposits. As with the suspected truncation, the date at which this occurred is not clear. The colluvium produced virtually no Romano-British pottery and no medieval or post-medieval material was recovered from it. Burnt flint and very friable fragments of late Bronze Age or early Iron Age pottery were distributed throughout the deposit.

A number of features were recorded cutting the colluvium, all datable to the nineteenth century or later. Many of these probably related to the use of the site by the Walmer Brewery.

Discussion

As with the prehistoric occupation the excavation has located the northern extent of activity in the Roman period, delimited to the north, in the earlier phase, by the presence of boundary ditches beyond which no identifiable activity was present. The alignment of the ditches clearly indicates that occupation extended to the west under the garden of No 246 Dover Road, and to the east where, as with the prehistoric activity, it became difficult to trace. Although the evidence is limited the morphology of the site suggests that the principal areas of occupation must have lain up slope to the south of the excavation area. Definition of the site limits in the later phase is less clear. The early boundary ditches had been sealed beneath redeposited soils. However the cutting of the east return of the L-shaped ditch on the same alignment as the earlier boundary implies the survival of the earlier boundary in some form, either as a fence or a hedge. This continuity of boundary is supported by the absence of Romano-British activity in the north of the excavation area and in watching brief and evaluation across the remainder of the site.

Any discussion of the chronology or morphology of the site is severely restricted by the limited area of activity observed in the excavation. The pottery indicates that occupation began in the first century AD and, though no close date can be put on this, it has been suggested that there is nothing to indicate that it began before the Roman conquest (*see* p 55). The presence of a La Tène III style pin brooch, dated to the first century BC or first century AD in pit 517 does not necessarily contradict this as the item could still have been in circulation, though unfashionable, into the second century AD or later.

The nature of the early Romano-British activity is unclear. Around forty-five pits have been suggested to belong to this period and, as noted elsewhere, a number of the pits forming the prehistoric pit complexes may also be of this date. The majority of the identified pits are consistent with a function as post-holes, though none was clearly proven to be so. The remainder had no obvious function and there is little to be gained from their discussion. Of those pits suggested to be post-holes only four could be associated and the nature of this association is unclear. The presence of cut features, domestic pottery and small quantities of animal bone suggests that the site lies on the edge of settlement, but the nature of this in this early phase is unknown. There is nothing in the finds assemblage to suggest a particularly high status to the site and so it cannot be determined whether we are dealing with an isolated farmstead, a villa or nucleated settlement of some sort. Small quantities of cereal and chaff recovered from sampling indicate agricultural activity, but these are not securely datable and could be either Iron Age or later Roman in date.

The arrangement of the earliest phase of boundary ditches suggests an entrance to the settlement in the dog-leg formed between their terminal ends. However the excavation provided little further evidence to support this suggestion in the form of structures, metalling or wear patterns. The ditches themselves do not appear to have been substantial and may have served for drainage and/or boundary rather than defensive purposes. The cutting of a single length of ditch across the site on the alignment of the southern ditch of the earlier boundary suggests that the causeway between the earlier ditches was no longer required, perhaps indicating changes of land use around the settlement or of arrangements within the settlement. The alterations also suggest that space was not at a premium within the boundary, as the new ditch reduced the area enclosed. The dating evidence is too limited to give an accurate chronology for the cutting and modification of the boundary, but it would seem that it occurred in the second century.

The burials of the child and horse close to the boundary were assumed during excavation to belong to this period. However there is evidence to suggest that the horse at least may be earlier. The relationship between the child and the horse burials was not clear, if they were even contemporary. The alignment of the graves and the orientation of the burials was significantly different, as was the depth to which they had been cut. However their proximity does suggest a possible association. Subsequent watching brief work conducted in the area failed to pick up any trace of further burials and so it must be assumed that these are isolated features.

In the absence of grave goods or incidental finds the burial of the child has been assigned to the early Roman period on the grounds of its appearance and preservation. The apparent formal arrangement of the body, lying supine within a grave cut is more typical of the Roman period than the early to middle Iron Age. During the Roman period burial customs included both inhumation, often extended lying supine, and cremation, both found within cemeteries, small grave groups or in isolated locations. The burial customs of the early to middle Iron Age are less clear than those of earlier or later periods and in general fewer burials of this date have been identified (Cunliffe 1991b, 498–510). In the early part of the period cremation is thought to be the norm, with urned burials giving way to unurned burial and, by the fifth century, inhumation burials becoming more common. The inhumations of the period are often crouched or flexed and lying on their sides. However there is wide local variation and in the south-east many burials occur in disused storage pits or as dismembered body parts spread across sites suggesting less formality to burial, although this may belie the true nature of the rituals involved. By the late Iron Age extended burials are found, notably at the nearby cemetery at Mill Hill, Deal (Parfitt 1995a).

The dating of the horse burial to the early Roman period is more uncertain and there is stratigraphic evidence that it was earlier. The backfill of the burial produced some forty sherds of early to middle Iron Age pottery, along with a piece of fired clay, but no Romano-British material. Further a pit (589) partially truncating its upper extent produced forty-two sherds of pottery of the same date along with evidence to suggest a primary flint knapping episode (see p 62). These relatively large assemblages are significantly above the background level of prehistoric pottery and so suggest deposition in this period rather than redeposition of disturbed material. However, also retrieved from the later feature and from deposits thought to predate the horse burial were sherds of pottery apparently from a single pedestal foot vessel of mid first-century date; the majority of these came from pit 589. The distribution of pottery from this vessel entirely from the upper soils within the pit complex, is suspected to be the result of surface trampling and reworking of the soil in the early Roman period and it is clear from the archive that there was some difficulty in understanding the upper sequence during excavation. The evidence indicates that the horse burial can be no later than the early Romano-British period and its inclusion here is considered to be the safest interpretation of the data.

A change in use of the excavated area is indicated in the later second century or early third century AD by the accumulation of the heterogeneous soil horizon across much of the site, sealing the boundary ditches, which had probably already become infilled. The material used was mixed, but probably derived from the clearance of spoil and rubbish from elsewhere given the worn nature of the pottery retrieved from the deposit. The exact date of deposition is thus uncertain. The location of the deposit confined to the suggested hollow or valley head indicates that it was intended to fill this feature, perhaps for alterations to the site layout. However it could equally be that this area was simply a convenient place to dump material as it was not being utilised in this period. The duration of the dumping cannot be determined from the evidence available, but the unevenness of its upper surface and its increasingly colluvial nature to the east may indicate that it took place over some time and in an *ad hoc* fashion.

A more substantial change to the layout, and possibly the extent and status of the site, is indicated by the construction of the aisled building and the L-shaped ditch cutting the redeposited soil horizon. Aisled structures form a common element of villa sites in Britain, if not actually forming the main accommodation, and the presence of this building suggests that by the second century a villa was present at the site. The date of construction of the building is unclear,

but given the dating of the pottery recovered from the soil horizon it must have been built no earlier than the early third century AD. The absence of floors or other features means that the function of the building remains speculative.

The ditch adjacent to the building is assumed to form an enclosure to its east, the size of which cannot be determined. That the two are contemporary is suggested spatially. The ditch was of some size, and although possibly a drainage ditch, its function and the nature of use of the area enclosed are unknown. The ditch was at least partially backfilled intentionally as to its south it was filled by redeposited domestic refuse, while to the north and along the eastern return it appeared to have been filled by colluvium.

Charred cereal and other vegetable remains were recovered from deposits associated with the building and with the L-shaped ditch. Three samples provided significant quantities for further analysis. All produced evidence for cereal growing, with spelt wheat and hulled barley present in large quantities (see p 74). The evidence further suggests processing to have taken place with high quantities of chaff and low quantities of weed seeds present. Included among this material were several sprouted wheat seeds possibly indicating that malting was taking place at the site. Whether this material related directly to the use of the aisled building or to nearby contemporary structures remains unclear as the material was found in redeposited contexts, and the quantities found in these samples were much higher than in other samples taken in the excavation, even those from close to the building.

The duration of use of the building and the ditch cannot be determined with any accuracy. No deposits can be associated with the abandonment of the building, possibly due to truncation, and the backfill of the ditch is probably derived from redeposited material as the dating from pottery is largely consistent with that of the material through which it was cut. The small quantity of late Roman pottery recovered from the ditch and the soil horizon suggests the presence of some later occupation, though the material may be intrusive in these contexts. The nature of any later activity in this area would appear to have been non-intrusive given the absence of pits or ditches of a clearly late date. The evidence suggests that the settlement may have contracted or shifted its focus by the end of the third century and it is possible that it had been abandoned by this time.

3

The Finds

The prehistoric pottery

Barbara McNee

Introduction

A total of 1,969 sherds weighing 17,494g and with a mean sherd weight of 8.9g was subjected to detailed analysis. Pottery from the early to middle Iron Age forms the largest component of this assemblage, but there are also small quantities of very late Bronze Age pottery. The condition of the pottery is fair to poor, many sherds are small and abraded, but the assemblage also includes a range of featured sherds, which has enabled a more detailed decoration, form, and fabric type analysis to be undertaken. The material is derived from 122 contexts, which mainly comprised intensive pitting.

	Sherd count	Sherd weight (g)
End of late Bronze Age or earliest Iron Age	184	1870
Early to middle Iron Age	1579	15431
Indeterminate	206	193
Total	1969	17494

Table 1. Summary of pottery by sherd and weight.

Methodology

The pottery was recorded using the methodology set out by the Prehistoric Ceramics Research Group (1997). All sherds were assigned a fabric type after macroscopic examination and by using a binocular microscope (x10 power). The assemblage was divided into different fabric groups on the basis of the dominant inclusion types, and to a fabric type

based on the variation within the group. Density charts (PCRG 1997, appendix 3) were used to standardise assessment of the quantity of inclusion present within the pottery fabric. All sherds were counted and weighed to the nearest whole gram, and given a unique Pottery Record Number (PRN) for ease of reference. Diagnostic sherds were additionally assigned to a form and decorative scheme; other characteristics noted include individual sherd thickness, surface treatment, levels of abrasion, and evidence of use-wear. Featured sherds were recorded onto individual featured sherd record sheets, and key sherds were selected and illustrated. Parallel form types were sought from within, and also outside the Kent area, using published and unpublished material.

Chronology

Two ceramic phases were identified. Ceramic phase 1 (end of the late Bronze Age decorated phase or earliest Iron Age) accounted for 9.3 per cent of the overall assemblage. Ceramic phase 2 (early to middle Iron Age) accounted for 80.2 per cent of the overall assemblage. The remaining 10.5 per cent of the assemblage could not be identified with any degree of certainty and is described as indeterminate.

Taphonomy

The majority of the contexts (ninety-nine in total) produced only small quantities of pottery. However one context (269) produced a large assemblage of pottery (over 100 sherds). In addition there are twenty-two medium-sized assemblages (over thirty sherds): it is considered that a minimum of twenty-five sherds should be present in a context in order for a reliable estimation of phase to be achieved (PCRG 1997, 21).

Condition		Sherd count and percentage		Sherd weight (g) and percentage	
1	Surface treatments are completely worn and all sherd edges are worn	262	13.30	227	1.30
2	Surface treatments are worn but stil identifiable and all sherd edges are worn	754	38.30	6164	35.20
3	Surface treatments are worn but still identifiable; most of the sherd edges are worn, but at least one edge may be less worn	173	8.80	1868	10.70
4	Surface treatments are in reasonable condition; all sherd edges are worn	474	24.00	5490	31.40
5	Surface treatments are in reasonable condition; most of the sherd edges are worn but at least one sherd edge is less worn	294	15.00	3690	21.10
6	Surface treatments are in reasonable condition; sherd edges are generally fresh	12	0.60	55	0.30

Table 2. Summary of sherd condition by count and weight.

The condition of the pottery was assessed on a scale of 1 to 6 (Table 2). The table indicates that most of the pottery is in a fairly poor condition with high levels of wear on the sherd breaks. Surface treatments are still identifiable on many sherds, but few sherds can be considered to be in very good condition. The average sherd weight is quite low, and does not vary much over time. Within Ceramic phase 1 the average sherd weight is 10.2g and in Ceramic phase 2 the average sherd weight is 9.8g. Average sherd weights for contexts producing assemblages of over thirty sherds are consistently low, with the exception of pit 204, which produced an assemblage with a mean sherd weight of 19g. The significance of this is discussed below.

Fabric descriptions

Twenty-three different fabric types were identified which can be placed in seven groups on the basis of principal inclusion types (Table 3). The fabric groups established include a range of flint-tempered fabrics; two flint and organic fabrics; two flint and grog fabrics; two quartz fabrics; two quartz and organic fabrics; four quartz and flint fabrics; and two shell and flint fabrics. A small number of sherds were considered too fragmentary to be assigned to a fabric group. All flint fabric types contain calcined flints (burnt and crushed).

Flint types

F1: a fairly fine fabric containing (15 per cent) moderately sorted subangular flint mostly 0.25–0.5mm in size, with some larger pieces 1mm in size. The clay matrix is silty and micaceous; fracture is fine; surface feels fine to rough.

F2: a coarse fabric containing very common (30 per cent) poorly sorted subangular flint up to 4mm in size. The clay matrix is silty and micaceous; fracture is irregular; surface feels rough.

F3: a fairly coarse fabric containing moderate (10–15 per cent) poorly sorted subangular flint up to 4mm in size. The clay matrix is silty and micaceous, fracture is irregular, surface feels quite rough.

F4: a fairly fine fabric containing sparse (7 per cent) quite well sorted subangular flint mostly 0.5mm in size with very occasional pieces up to 3mm in size. The clay matrix is silty and micaceous; fracture is fine; surface feels smooth.

F5: a fine fabric containing common (25 per cent) well sorted subangular flint mostly 0.25–0.5mm in size, with some larger pieces 1mm in size. The clay matrix is silty and micaceous; fracture is fine; surface feels fine to rough.

F6: a fairly coarse fabric containing common (20–25 per cent) quite poorly sorted subangular flint up to 2mm in size. The clay matrix is silty and micaceous; fracture is irregular; surface feels smooth.

F7: a coarse fabric containing moderate (15 per cent) poorly sorted subangular flint up to 3mm in size, and sparse (5 per cent) poorly sorted rounded red iron ore. The clay matrix is silty and micaceous; fracture is irregular; surface feels rough.

F8: this is fairly coarse fabric containing moderate (15 per cent) poorly sorted subangular flint mostly 0.25–0.5mm in size, with some larger pieces 1–2mm in size. The clay matrix consists of very fine sand and is micaceous; fracture is quite fine; surface feels fine to rough.

F9: a very coarse fabric containing abundant (40 per cent) quite poorly sorted subangular flint 3mm in size. The clay matrix is silty and micaceous; fracture is hackly; surface feels rough.

Flint and organic types

FO1: a coarse fabric containing common (25 per cent) poorly sorted subangular flint up to 3mm in size, and common (20 per cent) poorly sorted linear voids and also organic inclusions up to 3mm in size. The clay matrix is silty and micaceous; fracture is irregular; surface feels rough.

FO2: a coarse fabric containing very common (30 per cent) moderately sorted subangular flint up to 1mm in size. The clay matrix is an organic rich clay containing abundant small pellets of organic material which is probably naturally occurring; fracture is irregular; surface feels rough.

Flint and grog types

FG1: quite a coarse fabric containing moderate (15 per cent) poorly sorted subangular flint up to 2mm in size, and sparse (3 per cent) subrounded grog 1mm in size. The clay matrix is silty and micaceous; fracture is irregular; surface feels rough.

FG2: quite a fine fabric containing common (25 per cent) quite well sorted subangular flint mostly 0.25mm in size, with some larger (1mm) pieces. The clay matrix is silty and micaceous; fracture is fine; surface feels smooth.

Quartz types

Q1: a fine fabric containing abundant (50 per cent) well sorted very fine glauconite and quartz sand, and rare (1–2 per cent) poorly sorted subangular flint 1mm in size. The fresh fracture is fine; surface feels smooth.

Q2: a fine fabric containing abundant (50 per cent) well sorted silt size glauconite and quartz sand, rare (2 per cent) poorly sorted subangular flint 1mm in size, and rare (2 per cent) poorly sorted fine grained limestone fragments. The fresh fracture is fine; surface feels smooth.

Quartz and organic types

QO1: a fine fabric containing abundant (50 per cent) well sorted silt-size quartz grains and rare (2 per cent) subangular flint up to 0.25mm in size. The clay matrix is an organic rich clay containing very common small pellets of organic material which is probably naturally occurring; fracture is fine; surface feels smooth.

QO2: a fairly fine fabric containing abundant (50 per cent) well sorted silt size quartz grains and sparse (5 per cent) subangular flint up to 2mm in size. The clay matrix is an organic rich clay containing very common small pellets of organic material which is probably naturally occurring; fracture is quite fine; surface feels smooth to rough.

Quartz and flint types

QF1: a fairly coarse fabric containing common (25 per cent) reasonably sorted subrounded quartz 0.5–1mm in size, and common (20 per cent) poorly sorted subangular flint up to 1mm in size. The clay matrix is silty; fracture is quite fine; surface feels smooth.

QF2: quite a fine fabric containing abundant (40 per cent) well sorted very fine glauconite and quartz sand, and moderate (10–15 per cent) well sorted subangular flint 0.5–1mm in size. The fracture is fine; surface feels quite rough.

QF3: quite a coarse fabric containing abundant (40 per cent) well sorted quartz sand 0.20mm in size, and moderate (15 per cent) poorly sorted subangular flint up to 4mm in size. The fresh fracture is irregular; surface feels rough.

QF4: quite a coarse fabric containing abundant (40 per cent) well sorted fine glauconite sand, and moderate (10–15 per cent) poorly sorted subangular flint up to 2mm in size. The fracture is irregular; surface feels quite rough.

Shell and flint types

SF1: this is a coarse fabric containing moderate (15 per cent) poorly sorted shell up to 3mm in size, and moderate (10 per cent) poorly sorted subangular flint up to 3mm in size. The clay matrix consists of fine sand, with some larger quartz grains 0.25mm in size; fracture is hackly; surface feels rough.

SF2: this is a coarse fabric containing moderate (10 per cent) poorly sorted shell up to 3mm in size, and moderate (10 per cent) poorly sorted subangular flint up to 10mm in size. The clay matrix is silty and micaceous; fracture is irregular; surface feels quite rough.

Clay and temper sources

The site is located on the dip slope of the North Downs (Geological Survey Sheet of Great Britain No 290). The underlying solid geology is Upper Chalk overlain by a drift deposit of Head Brickearth (Jarman 2006, 1). Geologically the Downlands pottery fabrics suggest reliance on locally available resources for ceramic production during the late Bronze Age and Iron Age. This conclusion is based on the Dean Arnold model of resource procurement, whereby the preferred territory of exploitation for both clay and temper is 1km or less, and the common range of exploitation is within 7km for clay, and 6–9km for temper (Arnold 1985, 54–5; Morris 1994a and b).

Flint, the main fabric tempering, could have been obtained locally from the Chalk, which contains nodular flints and flint bands (Shephard-Thorn 1988, 17). Head Brickearth is suitable for manufacture of bricks and was exploited for this purpose at a number of sites within the area, and consists predominantly of silt-grade quartz grains (*ibid*, 34). Thanet Beds occur just over 7km from the site and comprise glauconite, clays, silts and fine sands (*ibid*, 26). Thanet Beds and Brickearth deposits could have provided plenty of suitable potting clays, and it is interesting to note the similarity of the clay matrix in most of the fabric types. This suggests that much of the pottery produced at Downlands derived from the same clay source. A number of sherds were thin-sectioned and suggest that the potters were actually exploiting a variety of clay sources, but that clay sources producing coarse silty clays were especially popular.

Pottery containing shell may have come from the Woolwich Beds which occur just over 6km north of the site, or from the

Fabric	Sherd count and percentage		Sherd weight (g) and percentage	
F1	384	19.50	3667	21.00
F2	192	9.80	2263	13.00
F3	254	12.90	2383	13.70
F4	298	15.10	2999	17.10
F5	118	6.00	1181	6.80
F6	327	16.60	3068	17.50
F7	10	0.50	133	0.80
F8	44	2.20	354	2.00
F9	6	0.30	37	0.20
FO1	15	0.80	105	0.60
FO2	11	0.60	58	0.30
FG1	1	0.00	16	0.10
FG2	1	0.00	9	0.10
Q1	47	2.40	419	2.40
Q2	3	0.20	40	0.20
QO1	8	0.40	119	0.70
QO2	3	0.20	22	0.10
QF1	7	0.40	85	0.50
QF2	13	0.70	98	0.60
QF3	1	0.00	27	0.20
QF4	1	0.00	7	0.00
SF1	2	0.10	199	1.10
SF2	1	0.00	3	0.00
Indeterminate	222	11.30	202	1.10

Table 3. Sherd counts and weight according to fabric type.

Upper Chalk beds. The infrequent use of this type of fabric makes it an unusual addition to the Downlands repertoire. Two sherds (PRN 90 and PRN 402) were thin-sectioned and the shell inclusions could be mussel or cockle. The shell is quite worn and rounded and may be naturally occurring within the clay. Clay from the Woolwich Beds may have been particularly chosen to make these vessels. Three fabrics (Q1, Q2 and QF4) are glauconitic, and these clays may have derived from the Gault clays at Folkestone. Gault Clay contains highly glauconitic sandy clay (Dines *et al* 1954, 25).

Some pots have been made with clay that is rich in organic matter such as roots. The clay itself has been badly prepared, and it appears that little attempt has been made to remove the organic matter, assuming that the organic material is naturally occurring in the clay. This has resulted in the organic material burning out leaving lots of striations. Some of the material has also carbonised, and the core of the pottery has the appearance of containing tiny pieces of charcoal. Other sherds also contain tiny pebbles, and pieces of fine grained sedimentary rock, and again, no attempt has been made to remove these from the clay. One sherd possibly contains gypsum, which is a common sedimentary mineral frequently found near the sea.

There is little correlation between fabric groups and form types, although bowl types tend to be made with finer fabrics. This is often the case, as fine fabrics would have helped facilitate the production of vessels with thinner walls and burnished surfaces. Fabric type F5 is one of the finest fabrics in the Downlands assemblage, and has mainly been used to make burnished bowls. Flint-tempered wares are very popular, accounting for 82.9 per cent of the entire assemblage, and flint has also been added to fabrics, which contain additional inclusions such as grog, quartz and shell.

Flint type F9 is a very coarse fabric, and has been used to make pottery assigned to the late Bronze Age ceramic phase. Most of the other fabrics have also been employed to make pots from this phase, with the exception of the finer fabric types such as F5; Q2; QO1 and QF2. The use of shelly fabrics is generally quite rare in Bronze Age Kent, and tends to gain in popularity in the early Iron Age (McNee forthcoming). Shelly fabrics are particularly common during the early Iron Age in south-east Essex (Brown 1995b, 30), and a similar picture can be seen in Kent. Fabrics containing significant amounts of glauconite are also more common in the Iron Age. Generally speaking a greater variety of finer fabrics and the addition of sandy fabrics appear in the late Bronze Age and early Iron Age Kent, and this would appear to be the case at Downlands. However, some of the fabric types cannot be placed within a chronological parameter, and it may be argued that there is an overlap and continuation of certain fabric recipes used by Bronze Age and Iron Age potters. Early Iron Age pots are often quite large, and coarse flinty fabrics were employed to make these vessels.

Vessel forms

Twenty-one rim form types, five or possibly six base types, and two angled shoulder types have been defined for the Downlands assemblage (Table 4). A number of sites were examined for parallels of the various vessel types. Parallels have also been sought outside of the Kent area in order to compare ceramic styles, and therefore contribute to a picture of social contact and ceramic influences.

Rim forms

R1: flat-topped rim with expanded outer edge; probably a straight-sided or slightly barrel-shaped pot (Fig 32, Nos 1–3).
Form type: ovoid jar.
Parallels: Saltwood Tunnel (Jones 2006a, no 74); North Shoebury (Wymer and Brown 1995, fig 67, 124 and fig 68, 131); Highstead (Couldrey 2007, fig 82, 288).

R2: flat-topped rim, long fairly upright neck joining a shoulder (Fig 32, Nos 1, 4, 5).
Form type: shouldered bowl.
Parallels: Saltwood Tunnel (Jones 2006a, no 65).

R3: round-topped rim, possible ovoid jar although orientation is difficult (not illustrated).
Form type: jar.
Parallels: White Horse Stone (Morris 2006, no 117).

R4: flaring beaded rim (Fig 32, No 6).
Form type: bowl.
Parallels: White Horse Stone (Morris 2006, no 146).

R5: round-topped rim, long flaring neck (Fig 32, Nos 7–11).
Form type: carinated bowl.
Parallels: Whitfield–Eastry by-pass Site 2 (Macpherson-Grant 1997, 68); Saltwood Tunnel (Jones 2006a, no 55 and 75); White Horse Stone (Morris 2006, no 123); Danebury (Brown 2000, 107, fig 3.29); Dolland's Moor (Macpherson-Grant 1990, 61).

R6: flat-topped rim, long inverted neck joining a carinated shoulder (Fig 32, No 13).
Form type: carinated bowl.
Parallels: Dumpton Gap (Bryan 2002); White Horse Stone (Morris 2006, no 65); Highstead (Couldrey 2007, fig 84, 299).

R7: round-topped rim with slight internal bead, long upright neck joining a shoulder (Fig 32, No 14).
Form type: probably a bowl.
Parallels: Saltwood Tunnel (Jones 2006a, no 33); White Horse Stone (Morris 2006, no 140).

R8: flat-topped rim, possibly fairly straight sided (Fig 32, No 15).
Form type: uncertain.
Parallels: Saltwood Tunnel (Jones 2006a, no 74).

R9: flat-topped rim, long inverted neck joining a shoulder, similar to form type R6 but burnished on the interior only (Fig 32, No 16).
Form type: bowl or jar.
Parallels: Dumpton Gap (Bryan 2002).

R10: flat-topped rim, long upright neck joining a gentle rounded shoulder (Fig 32, Nos 17–18).
Form type: jar.
Parallels: Chanctonbury Ring (Hamilton 2001, fig 11:4);

Chalk Hill, Ramsgate (McNee forthcoming); Ellington School (McNee 2007, fig 4,34); North Shoebury (Wymer and Brown 1995, 84, fig 65.95).

R11: round-topped 'thickened' everted rim, fairly long neck (Fig 32, Nos 19–20).
Form type: jar.
Parallels: Dumpton Gap (Bryan 2002); Danebury (Brown 2000, 98, fig 3.20).

Context	Group	Description	R1	R2	R3	R4	R5	R6	R7	R8	R9	R10	R11	R12	R13	R14	R15	R16	R17	R18	R19	R20	R21	B1	B4
203	9	prehistoric rubbish pit																							1
206	2	prehistoric pit													1										
211	2	prehistoric ditch							1																
213	2	prehistoric ditch														1									
269	3	prehistoric linear hollow	1	1	1	1																		1	
475	21	early Roman pit								1								1							
480	24	middle Roman surface finds	1																						
507	12	prehistoric pit												1	1		1								
511	12	prehistoric pit		1																					
516	21	prehistoric pit										1													
525	3	early Roman pit																	1						
552	12	prehistoric pit		1						1														1	
560	8	prehistoric pit																1							
581	12	early Roman pit											1												
584	12	prehistoric pit																				1			
588	20	early Roman pit																					1		
615	12	prehistoric pit																1							
624	12	prehistoric pit										1				1									
625	12	prehistoric rubbish pit													1									1	
634	8	prehistoric pit																							
690	14	early Roman colluvium													2	2									
713	10	prehistoric pit												1											
728	12	prehistoric pit																		1					
735	12	prehistoric pit												1											
738	4	prehistoric pit																			1				
800	21	early Roman pit	1				1					1				1	1								
833	21	early Roman pit										2													
835	10	prehistoric pit				1																			
845	10	prehistoric pit				2				1															
907	21	early Roman pit	1				3	1	1	1															
913	10	prehistoric pit												1											
surface					1																			

Table 4. Fabric type by context.

47

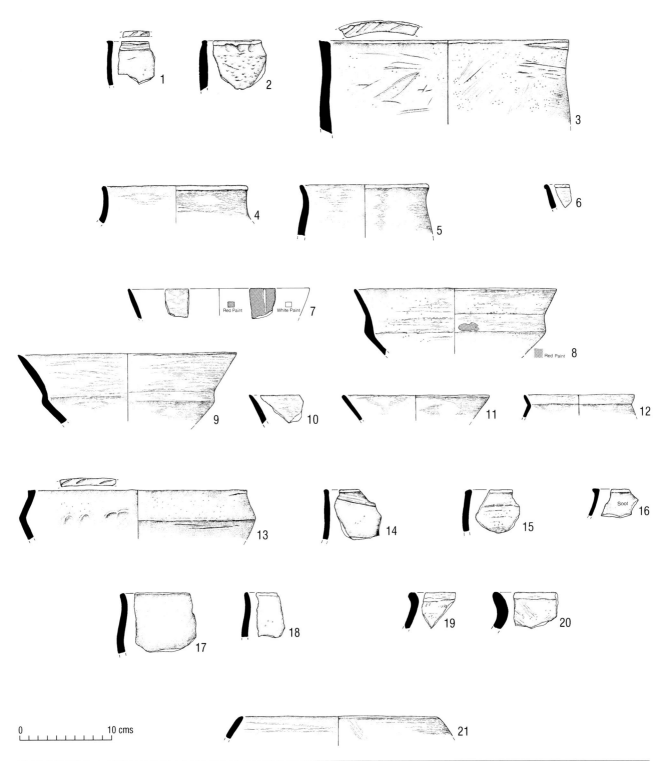

0 [_____] 10 cms

Fig 32. Rim forms R1–R12. **1**: jar with 'pie-crust' decoration, fabric F1, context 269, PRN 2; **2**: jar, fabric F6, context 800, PRN 165; **3**: jar with 'pie-crust' decoration, fabric F6, context 480, PRN 200; **4**: burnished bowl, fabric F3, context 907, PRN 25; **5**: shouldered bowl, fabric F1, context 511, PRN 288; **6**: bowl, fabric F1, context 269, PRN 14; **7**: haematite on exterior, fabric Q2, context 907, PRN 20; **8**: burnished bowl, fabric F1, context 907, PRN 21; **9**: carinated bowl, fabric F4, context 835, PRN 46, 47; **10**: Rim sherd from a long necked bowl. Fabric F4, context 845, PRN 66; **11**: long necked bowl, fabric F4, context 800, PRN 164; **12**: Rim sherd from a short necked shouldered bowl, fabric F4, context 713, PRN 313; **13**: burnished bowl with 'pie-crust' decoration, fabric F6, context 907, PRN 23; **14**: long-necked vessel, fabric F3, context 907, PRN 24; **15**: ovoid vessel, fabric F2, context 907, PRN 26; **16**: sooting on exterior, fabric F4, context 835, PRN 51; **17**: shouldered jar, fabric F6, context 833, PRN 77; **18**: shouldered jar, fabric F3, context 516, PRN 301; **19**: sooting on exterior, fabric F01, context 507, PRN 106: **20**: grass impressions on surface, fabric F3, context 581, PRN 292; **21**: possible bowl, fabric F2, context 507, PRN 107. Scale 1:4.

R12: flat-topped rim, convex profile (Fig 32, No 21).
Form type: bowl.
Parallels: Dumpton Gap (Bryan 2002); Saltwood Tunnel (Jones 2006a, no 62).

R13: round-topped slightly flaring short rim (Fig 33, Nos 22–4).
Form type: bowl.
Parallels: Dumpton Gap (Bryan 2002); Danebury (Brown 2000, 107, fig 3.29; Highstead (Couldrey 2007, fig 84, 299).

R14: round-topped slightly everted short rim (Fig 33, No 23).
Form type: jar.
Parallels: Dumpton Gap (Bryan 2002).

R15: flat-topped rim, gentle barrel shape, similar to R1 although the outer edge of the rim is flatter (Fig 33, No 26–7).
Form type: jar.
Parallels: Saltwood Tunnel (Jones 2006a, no 27); White Horse Stone (Morris 2006, no 76); Whitfield–Eastry by-pass (Macpherson-Grant 1997, 67); Highstead (Couldrey 2007, fig 82, 297).

R16: round-topped rim, long flaring neck joining a carinated shoulder. This is very similar to R5 although the neck is more concave and can be slightly shorter (Fig 33, No 28).
Form type: bowl.
Parallels: Rectory Road, Essex (Hamilton 1988, fig 68.6); Danebury (Brown 2000, 107, fig 3.29; Saltwood Tunnel (Jones 2006a, nos 61 and 65).

R17: round-topped 'thickened' outcurving rim (Fig 33, Nos 29–30).
Form type: possibly a simple hemispherical bowl.
Parallels: Danebury (Brown 2000, 109, fig 3.30); Beechbrook Wood (Jones 2006b, no 20).

R18: round-topped rim (Fig 33, No 31).
Form type: possibly a simple open bowl.
Parallels: White Horse Stone (Morris 2006, nos 52 and 53); Beechbrook Wood (Jones 2006b, no 14); Ellington School (McNee 2007, fig 4, 41).

R19: flat-topped rim, short upright neck, joining a shoulder (Fig 33, No 32).
Form type: bowl?
Parallels: Dumpton Gap (Bryan 2002); Highstead (Couldrey 2007, fig 82, 291); Danebury (Brown 2000, 89, fig 3.31).

R20: rounded barrel shape, necked short rim (Fig 33, No 33).
Form type: bowl.
Parallels: Ebbsfleet (Macpherson-Grant 1992, 90, fig 6); White Horse Stone (Morris 2006, no 71).

R21: possible shoulderless open bowl or lid (not illustrated).
Parallels: Dumpton Gap (Bryan 2002).

Ceramic phase 1: very late Bronze Age or very earliest Iron Age forms

The following form types are present: R3; R7; R10; R13; R14 and R18. Rims are small and worn, and it has not been possible to calculate any of the rim diameters. These form types can be quite long lived, and continue into the Iron Age and are therefore not reliable chronological indicators. However, form type R18 is a hemispherical bowl, and these appear to be more common throughout the late Bronze Age. The pottery from phase 1 is characterised by quite coarse, thick walled vessels, which can have a crumbly texture, and is considered to be slightly earlier than the rest of the assemblage, or representative of an intermediary stage. There are five R10 shouldered jar sherds (Fig 32, Nos 17–18), and these are closely comparable to jars found at Ramsgate (McNee forthcoming), and Chanctonbury Ring (Hamilton 2001). Both these sites are best described as belonging to the decorated phase of the late Bronze Age as defined by Barrett (1980), and approximately dating to the eighth to seventh century BC.

Ceramic phase 1 includes one splayed base sherd (B3) (Fig 34, No 40), and three flat-bottomed base sherds (B2). Two sherds (B2) have a flint gritted underbase, and this may indicate that manufacture of the pot was carried out on a bed of burnt and crushed flint to stop the base of the pots from sticking (Macpherson-Grant 1991, 39). This method of manufacture appears on numerous sites in Kent, and may start as early as 1100 BC, or even earlier, and continue up to and possibly beyond 600 BC.

The use of finger 'kneading' is evident on one body sherd (PRN 358; context 340, not illustrated) and could be a result of the use of finger squeezing to form and finish vessel shapes that have been slab built (Hamilton 1987, 58). Rippling on the exterior surfaces of vessels is a feature, which remained common among the seventh century BC groups in eastern and south coast Britain (Bradley and Ellison 1975). It is evident that some of the Downlands pots have been constructed by slab building as well as coil building. Three sherds are decorated, one rim sherd (R14; PRN 170; context 800, not illustrated) has 'pie crust' decoration on top of the shoulder; one rounded shoulder sherd has been decorated with tiny finger impressions, possibly belonging to a child, and one sherd has a single horizontal incised line made with a sharp tool of some description.

Surface treatment is confined to simple wiping and burnishing, and eighty-two sherds from phase 1 do not appear to have any form of surface treatment. This is in contrast to pottery from phase 2, when a wealth of surface treatments appears. This is discussed in more detail below.

Ceramic phase 2: early to middle Iron Age

This is characterised by jars and bowls. All forms are present with the exception of form type R3, and R18. There are

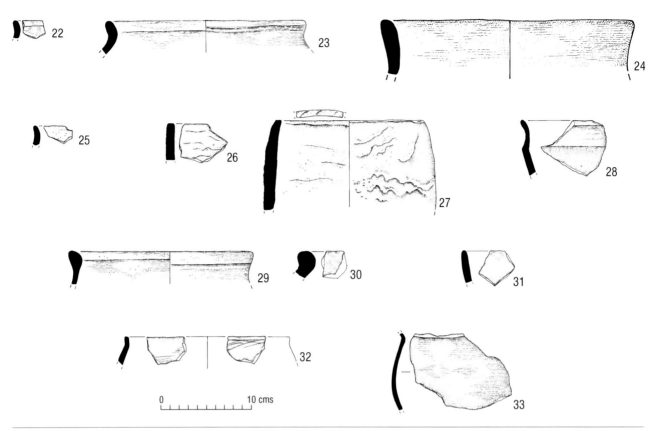

Fig 33. Rim forms R13–R20. **22**: bowl, fabric QF1, context 690, PRN 121; **23**: bowl, fabric F1, context 735, PRN 224; **24**: bowl, fabric Q1, context 625, PRN 235. Scale 1:4. **25**: jar, fabric QF2, context 690, PRN 123; **26**: jar, exterior rusticated, fabric F2, context 507, PRN 108; **27**: rusticated jar with possible 'pie-crust' decoration on top of rim, fabric F1, context 213, PRN 143; **28**: carinated bowl, fabric F4, context 800, PRN 163; **29**: bowl, fabric F6, context 475, PRN 182; **30**: bowl, Fabric F7, context 560, PRN 329; **31**: bowl, fabric F3, context 525, PRN 274; **32**: fabric F6, context 728, PRN 311; **33**: round-bodied bowl, fabric F4, context 738, PRN 167. Scale 1:4.

similarities between some of the form types, which could be variations on a theme, or the work of the same potter. Form types tend to fall into five main groups: shouldered jars; neckless ovoid jars; long necked shouldered bowls; short necked shouldered bowls and closed bowls. Shouldered jars are common components of late Bronze and Iron Age sites, and ovoid jars are very long-lived vessels, which can date from as early as the middle Bronze Age, through to the middle Iron Age. Neckless ovoid jar types R1, R8, and R15, are similar although R8 is burnished possibly inside and form type is uncertain. Two examples of form type R1 have 'pie crust' decoration on top of the rim, and two type R15 jars have 'rustication' on the exterior (see surface treatment for full discussion). Ovoid shaped jars with rusticated surfaces are well paralleled from a number of sites in Kent, including Saltwood Tunnel (Jones 2006a, no 27), Highstead (Macpherson-Grant 1991, 40), and Whitfield–Eastry by-pass (Macpherson-Grant 1997, 67).

Long necked carinated bowls tend to dominate the Downlands assemblage, and form types R5 and R16 are very similar. R2; R4 and R7 might also belong to this group, although with no surviving shoulders it is difficult to say. Similar bowls have been found at other sites, for example Danebury (Brown 2000, fig 3.29, type BA 2.2 and BA 2.3), and have been dated to the fifth to fourth century BC. There are also good parallels at White Horse Stone, and these have

been phased to the early to middle Iron Age (Morris 2006). One small rim sherd (type R5) is coated in red haematite on the exterior, and possible traces of white paint (Fig 32, No 7). This rim sherd probably belongs to a long necked carinated bowl, and is therefore similar to vessels from Whitfield–Eastry by-pass (Macpherson-Grant 1997, 68).

There is only one example of form type R21 that is possibly a lid, and is similar to a vessel from Dumpton Gap, which may also be a lid (Bryan 2002). Form type R17 is similar to bowl type BC1 from Danebury, which belongs to cp 4-7, 360 BC onwards (Brown 2000, 89). There are three R17 rims present in the Downlands assemblage, which may indicate continuation into the middle Iron Age. Form type R11 is also similar to Danebury jar type JC2.1, cp 5-7, 350 BC onwards (*ibid*, 87). There are however not enough sherds present within the assemblage to be sure of this.

Base forms and angled shoulder forms

B1: foot-ring base with flaring wall (Fig 34, Nos 34–6).

B2: flat-bottomed base with slightly flaring walls (Fig 34, Nos 37–9).

B3: splayed base (Fig 34, Nos 40–1).

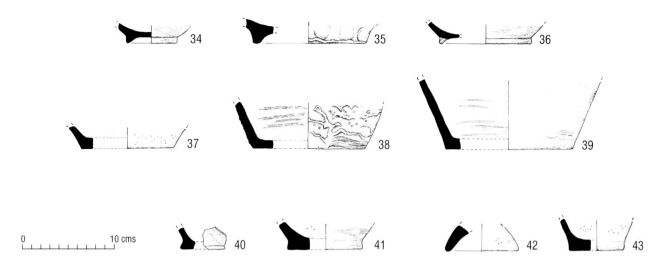

Fig 34. Base forms B1–B5. **34**: pedestal, fabric F1, context 269, PRN 1; **35**: foot-ring, fabric F6, context 588, PRN 202; **36**: fabric F4, context 552, PRN 267; **37**: base sherd with flaring walls, fabric F2, context 204, PRN 97; **38**: rusticated vessel, fabric F1, context 269, PRN 6; **39**: fabric F4, context 845, PRN 64; **40**: fabric F1, context 269, PRN 9; **41**: thick-walled, fabric F4, context 588, PRN 203; **42**: pedestal, fabric f1, context 216, PRN 203; **43**: small vessel, fabric F6, context 575, PRN 317. Scale 1:4.

B4: pedestal base (Fig 34, No 42).

B5: flat-bottomed base with fairly upright walls (Fig 34, No 43).

B6: possible omphalos base.

B7: central disc only/unclassified base.

A1: carinated shoulder.

A2: rounded shoulder.

Most of the surviving bases from Downlands are flat-bottomed with flaring walls, and span both ceramic phases. Some of the bases have snapped off from the vessel wall, indicating inadequate coil joining. Ceramic phase 2 at Downlands sees the introduction of a small number of foot-ring and pedestal bases, and these can be found on a number of Kentish sites including the early Iron Age phase at Highstead (Macpherson-Grant 1991, 42).

Several shoulder sherds survive; most of these are quite nicely burnished and probably relate to bowl forms. Two rounded shoulder sherds have been heavily rusticated, and are similar to pots from Highstead (*ibid*).

Surface treatment

Fourteen types of surface treatment were identified within the assemblage (see Table 5). Some form of surface treatment is evident on 1,191 sherds (60.5 per cent); an additional thirty sherds may have been burnished but are very worn,

Surface treatment	Sherd count and percentage		Sherd weight	Additional information
basal flints	4	0.20	52	appears in ceramic phase 1 only
burnishing	723	36.70	5852	mostly all over burnishing
Rustication 1	34	1.70	583	rustication on exterior
Rustication 1 and burnishing	122	6.20	1870	rustication on exterior, burnishing on interior
Rustication 1 and wiping	77	3.90	1246	rustication on exterior, wiping on interior
Rustication 2 and burnishing	4	0.20	142	rustication on exterior, burnishing on interior
Rustication 2 and wiping	1	0.05	56	rustication on exterior, wiping on interior
simple wiping	164	8.30	2507	some evidence of grass wiping
applied clay slurry/wiped	1	0.05	41	wiping quite rough, almost rusticated
finger wiping	3	0.20	160	mostly vertical finger wiping on the exterior of the vessel
haematite or red-finished	3	0.20	22	traces of red paint on exterior of rim
finger 'kneading'	1	0.05	52	exterior of pot has been 'kneaded', occurs in ceramic phase 1
smoothing	31	1.60	577	
surfact 'combing' or possibly Rustication 3	23	1.20	247	shallow to deep combing impressions

Table 5. Summary of surface treatments by sherd count and weight (cermaic phases 1 and 2).

and the remaining pottery sherds display no obvious surface treatments.

The most common form of surface treatment at Downlands is burnishing. This technique occurs in both ceramic phases and gives a surface lustre, which varies from a fine polish, to quite a rough 'random' uneven burnish. Most of the pots have been burnished on the exterior and interior which is both a functional and decorative treatment. It gives the vessel a smooth polished surface, and also reduces the permeability of the pot (Gibson 2002, 65). This would indicate that some of the pots from Downlands were used to contain liquid.

Pots with 'rusticated' surfaces account for 12.5 per cent of the entire assemblage. Macpherson-Grant highlights the significance of 'rustication', which is a surface treatment peculiar to east Kent and the Continent in the early to middle Iron Age (Macpherson-Grant 1991, 41–3; Couldrey 2007, 170). There are three types of rustication at Downlands; it may also be argued that surface combing is a type of rustication.

Rustication 1: clay slurry has been applied to the exterior surface and 'roughened', creating an encrusted effect.

Rustication 2: clay slurry has been applied to the exterior surface and 'scratched' on.

Rustication 3: the exterior surface has been 'combed'.

Rustication type 1 occurs on many sites in Kent, including Dumpton Gap (Bryan 2002), White Horse Stone (Morris 2006) and Ebbsfleet (Macpherson-Grant 1992). The clay slurry has been applied quite thickly on most vessels possibly using fingers and a tool of some description. A number of rusticated sherds have been thin-sectioned and strands of organic material within the slurry itself might suggest that a pad of grass was also used. Finger smears are evident on a few vessels, and marks from a wide comb on another. Other vessels have 'peaks' and 'blobs' of slurry, and it is tentatively suggested that these were applied using a sponge. Reasons for this dramatic surface finish are open to discussion, but it is interesting to note that most of the rusticated pots have been burnished inside, and may have held liquid. Some of the pots were thick walled and probably quite large, and the rough surface could have provided a better grip during transportation. Another possibility is that the pots functioned as large cooking vessels. Experiments have shown that a rough exterior provides more escape routes for steam, and helps prevent spalling during cooking. A heavy exterior texture is a technological choice available to the potter seeking to reduce thermal cracking (Skibo and Schiffer 1995, 83). One rusticated sherd from Downlands has sooting on the exterior, which would suggest that it has been used in a cooking activity.

At White Horse Stone rustication has been found on all sizes and thicknesses of vessel (Morris 2006). Morris suggests that if rustication was only found on large vessels

it could be interpreted as providing an anti-slippage effect. However, this technique is not present on large vessels in other areas, and may be a 'style statement' for the early to middle Iron Age Kent (ibid). It has not been possible to calculate the actual size of the Downlands rusticated pots, but wall thicknesses have been measured and vary from 5mm up to 15mm. This suggests that rustication was also applied to smaller pots.

One body sherd is of interest. It has been heavily rusticated, and then sprinkled with fine flint and pieces of crushed grog. Although grog is used as a temper in late Bronze Age and early Iron Age sites in Kent, it is the flint-tempered fabrics that dominate. Grog is an ideal tempering material, it is easily crushed, provides a stable non-plastic, which, on firing, has properties almost identical to the clay matrix, and does not suffer post-firing changes, which would destabilise the pot (Cleal 1995, 192). The overall picture of grog as an unpopular choice of inclusion may be indicative of social constraints on its use (ibid), and explain why it is not used as widely as other fabrics. The use of grog is very rare at Downlands, so it seems odd that the potter chose to coat a rusticated sherd in pieces of grog and flint. The sherd is even more visually striking than the rest of the rusticated pots, and may have been a special pot or family heirloom. It is interesting to observe that tiny sherds of grog can be seen in some of the thin sections of rusticated pots. It is possible that the potter may have had a pile of grog ready to be used as a temper for other pottery, and that the incorporation of small pieces of grog into the rusticated pots was accidental. However, it may also add to the argument that rusticated pots were intended to be 'style statements', and representative of a 'cultural' zone (Macpherson-Grant 1990, 63), and the inclusion of grog is representative of family histories.

Rustication type 2 occurs on just five sherds. The applied clay slip appears to be thinner than the slip used for rustication type 1, and the scratch marks appear on the body of the pot. A thin pointed tool may have been used, and it is also evident that the clay slurry has been applied using grass or straw. Rustication type 3 occurs on twenty-three sherds, and may also be a decorative technique. The exterior of the pot has been 'combed', and includes quite deep evenly spaced horizontal combing, and narrow combing which appears to have been quite randomly applied. This technique is similar to pottery found at Dolland's Moor (Macpherson-Grant 1990, 62, photograph bottom left), and Beechbrook (Jones 2006b, no 99). 'Combed' pots may have been intended for rustication, as scoring the exterior of the pot would have created a surface which would enable the application of clay slurry to adhere more efficiently.

The production of rusticated pots would have been quite time consuming, in particular pots that have been both burnished and rusticated. It is possible that the burnishing of the pot and application of the slurry would have taken place at different stages. The slurry may have been applied first as the pot would need to be damp and possibly scored in order for the slurry to adhere to the surface. A vessel intended for burnishing must be at the right stage of leather hardness, so

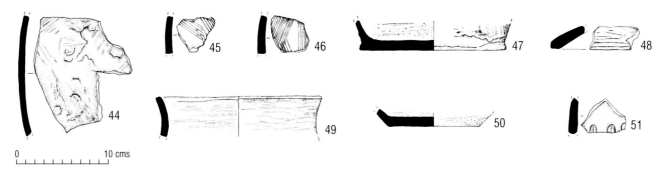

Fig 35. Surface treatment and decoration. **44**: rustication type 2, fabric F1, context 850, PRN 37; **45**: 'combing', fabric F4, context 850, PRN 39; **46**: 'combing', fabric F4, context 845, PRN 70; **47**: rustication, fabric F3, context 569, PRN 160; **48**: deep combing or burnish marks, fabric F6, context 590, PRN 222; **49**: burnished bowl, fabric Q01, context 269, PRN 4; **50**: small base sherd, burnished interior and exterior, fabric F6, context 690, PRN 125; **51**: finger-impressed decoration, fabric F1, context 850, PRN 36. Scale 1:4.

this may have taken place after the pot had been rusticated (Dr Sandy Budden, pers comm).

Wiping and smoothing are common types of surface treatment, and several sherds have grass impressions on the surface indicating the use of grass or straw to wipe the vessel. Another sherd was wiped with fingers. Three sherds are coated in red haematite (Fig 32, No 7), and it has become apparent that these wares are widespread in Kent and southern England (Middleton 1995, 203–4). Two sherds were thin sectioned (PRN 20 and 210). The clay derived from two different clay source and different techniques were employed to produce the red finish. PRN 20 has a sandy slightly glauconitic clay matrix, and the haematite appears to have been burnished into the surface of the bowl. This technique is similar to an example found at Highstead, and would have required a hard surface (Couldrey 2007, 166). PRN 210 is a silty flint-tempered pot, and the haematite has been applied as a slip. The surface of the pot is fairly uneven, causing small pockets of haematite. Previous research suggests that the production and distribution of red-finished pottery may not have been centralised, but that the manufacture was in some way specialised (*ibid*, 209). The red-finished pots from Downlands suggest local rather than centralised production. These vessels are quite distinct, however, and may have been traded.

Decoration

The Downlands assemblage is largely undecorated, and only eighteen sherds (0.9 per cent) display any form of decoration. Five rim sherds (form types R1; R6: and R14) have 'pie-crust' decoration on top of the rim. One (R15) jar (Fig 33, No 27) may also have faint 'pie-crust' decoration. 'Pie-crust' decoration occurs in the Bronze Age, and continues into the Iron Age. The Downlands 'pie-crust' rims are quite crude, and suggest that the potters did not want to spend much time carefully decorating the pottery. The decoration also appears to have been made with some form of flat tool rather than the fingertips. Three sherds have a row of finger-tip impressions on the exterior of the vessel. The finger-tips on one of these

examples are tiny, and may indicate that a child was involved in making the pot. Eight small body sherds from the same pot have a single horizontal tooled line. The lack of decorated pots is consistent with other sites in Kent dated to the early to middle Iron Age, for example Saltwood Tunnel (Jones 2006a) and Dumpton Gap (Bryan 2002). It is interesting to note that on other Kentish early to middle Iron Age sites, the demise of decorative techniques seems to coincide with the proliferation of surface treatments and it may be argued that the decorative additions to the surface of the pot took place through surface treatments. Combed impressions (discussed above) may have been both aesthetically pleasing as well as contributing to the functional efficiency of a vessel.

Firing

Vessels were generally irregularly fired and have a blotchy coloured surface, which is indicative of a short firing time in an open bonfire or pit. Fineware bowls tend to be completely unoxidised, implying deliberate and skilful management of fuel and firing techniques. A very small percentage of sherds are completely oxidised, also suggesting that the potters were able to maintain control of firing mechanisms. Fuel, in this case, would need to burn very rapidly and draw a steady rush of oxygen through the fire setting. The wood would need to be very dry and free of resin, and suggests careful storage of fuel (Dr Sandy Budden, pers comm).

Discussion of features

Prehistoric boundary ditches (G2)

Pottery recovered from this group of ditches would appear to be fairly contemporary. Ditch 212/220 produced one rim sherd (type R7), and four other sherds, which have been dated to the late Bronze Age decorated phase. This ditch was replaced by ditch 208/226/228, which also contained sherds of late Bronze Age pottery. Rusticated pottery was found in ditch sections 212/220; 214 and 216, including a rusticated type R15 jar (Fig 33, No 27). One very worn angled sherd with haematite coating derived from ditch section 224, and probably belongs to a shouldered bowl. Red-finished pottery occurs in both late Bronze Age and early Iron Age assemblages (Middleton 1995). The presence of both late Bronze Age and Iron Age pottery in some of these ditches suggests a co-existence of pottery styles, and a long history of use, and it is doubtful whether particular styles of potting tradition ended abruptly. Rustication first appears in the early Iron Age (Macpherson-Grant 1992, 291); there is however an argument for rustication appearing at Little Stock Farm, Mersham in the late Bronze Age/earliest Iron Age. This would suggest that the currently accepted date for this phenomenon needs to be slightly earlier (Bryan 2006, 10). The ceramic evidence for G2 suggests a very late Bronze Age and/or earliest Iron Age date, and the abrasion on pottery deriving from ditch sections 212/220 and 208/226/228 is particularly worn.

Irregular linear hollow with burnt flint spread (G3)

Pits 284 and 283 produced twelve sherds of coarse crumbly late Bronze Age pottery, which is in very poor condition. A good assemblage of early Iron Age pottery derived from the burnt flint layer 269, including a foot-ring base (Fig 34, No 34), numerous rusticated sherds, one jar with 'pie-crust' decoration (Fig 32, No 1), and two bowl forms (R2 and R4, Fig 35, No 49 and Fig 32, No 6).

Pit complex 1: early pits (G4)

Pits assigned to this group may belong to the earliest phases of occupation on the site (Jarman 2006, 11). One heavily abraded sherd has a 'kneaded' surface (discussed above) and may be late Bronze Age; the remaining twenty sherds are mostly rusticated. One large sherd was found with a fragment of human skull in pit 328, and had been rusticated (type 2). The edges are fairy worn, and although the sherd may have been deliberately deposited, it was probably broken some time before deposition. It is similar to four sherds of pottery recovered from pits assigned to G10, which are also in this complex. One rounded body sherd was recovered from pit 739 (Fig 33, No 33) and is very similar to a carinated bowl from pit 918 (Fig 32, No 8). The surfaces of both sherds are worn, but may have been coated with haematite.

Pit complex 1: later pits (G10)

This pit complex produced a large assemblage of early to middle Iron Age pottery. It includes two carinated R5 bowls; a short necked shouldered bowl (Fig 32, No 12); a shoulderless jar (R15), and several rusticated sherds. Four sherds are very similar to pottery found in G4. Joining sherds from a carinated bowl (Fig 32, Nos 9 and 10) were found in contexts 835, 845 and 850, which come from pits 836 and 848/849/851/852. The edges on the joining sherds are quite worn; this may indicate that the pottery was exposed to weathering or trampling prior to ending up in their excavated

contexts. Pots from the same vessel, but found in different pits, may have derived from the same source, possibly a rubbish dump, which was then cleared into open pits. Pottery from these pit features is quite comparable with each other, and suggests a group of related material.

Pit complex 2: later pits in east pit complex (G12)

This pit complex produced a good assemblage of early to middle Iron Age pottery, characterised by rusticated jars and burnished bowls. Two rim sherds (R11, Fig 32, Nos 19–20), and one rim sherd (R17) may be slightly later as they are quite similar to pots from Danebury, which have been dated to ceramic phase 350 BC onwards. One rim type (R11) was recovered from the upper fill of pit 512, and this may suggest a later phase of prehistoric use in the east pit complex (Fig 32, No 19). It is possible that the complex was in use for a long period of time, as pits 623, 528 and 581 contained pottery that is characteristic of late Bronze Age wares. Some of the pottery is very coarse and crumbly, and 623 contained two rim sherds (type R10), which commonly occur from the late Bronze Age onwards.

Pits (G9) to the north of the prehistoric boundary

Sherds from a suspected cremation vessel (568) and backfill (567) are very fragmented, but include some rusticated sherds and a large sherd from a rusticated base (Fig 35, No 47). The base appears to have been roughly grass-wiped on the interior, and is in reasonable condition, suggesting breakage may have occurred quite soon before burial. The presence of rustication would indicate an early Iron Age date for this feature. Two pits, 203 and 205, contained a number of reasonably worn sherds including some rusticated sherds and a pedestal base (Fig 34, No 42). One rusticated sherd has been tempered with shell, which also suggests an early Iron Age date. However, a few sherds do appear slightly earlier (late Bronze Age). The wear on the pottery indicates that the vessels may have derived from a rubbish dump, which was then cleared into open pits. It is interesting to note that the average sherd weight (19g) for pit 215 is above average and that although the pottery is not in very good condition it is still less abraded than most of the pottery at Downlands. This might suggest that pottery from this particular pit may have derived from an area with possibly a concentrated rubbish source, which had not suffered random dispersal and trampling of the pottery.

Reworked soils (G14) over pit complexes

Early to middle Iron Age pottery was recovered from these pit complexes, and is again characterised by rusticated sherds; one red-finished sherd; one bowl (R13, Fig 33, No 22) and one jar (R14, Fig 33, No 25). The pottery is in a poor state and coated in limescale. This is not indicative of use-wear but rather the boggy conditions surrounding the pottery.

Pits (G21) cutting reworked soil

This produced quite a range of early to middle Iron Age bowls and jars including several rusticated sherds; three carinated bowls (R5), one or possibly two of these are coated in haematite (Fig 32, Nos 7–8); and one carinated bowl (R16, Fig 33, No 28). At least four (R10) jars were also recovered (Fig 32, Nos 17–18); this might suggest very late Bronze Age activity. R10 jars from pits 184 and 517 are particularly worn and have been made with a coarse fabric. One body sherd (PRN 304, not illustrated) recovered from pit 517 is quite similar to very late Bronze Age sherds from Ramsgate. The sherd has been roughly wiped in quite a decorative fashion, and is almost 'rusticated' but does not have the 'encrusted' effect that many rusticated sherds have. It is tentatively suggested that the Ramsgate examples may represent some form of transitional period from the end of the late Bronze Age into the Iron Age (McNee forthcoming). Pottery from 517 and Ramsgate do share similarities, and may therefore suggest a very late Bronze Age date.

One R10 jar, recovered from pit 801, is less abraded than other pottery from this pit and has a finer fabric. It is interesting to note that a type R5 bowl was also recovered and may suggest that this group of pottery is slightly later.

Levelling, terracing for Roman building and contemporary ditch (G23, G24 and G27)

Pottery recovered from these groups is in quite poor condition and has few diagnostic features. The presence of a number of rusticated sherds would suggest an early Iron Age date. One sherd from ditch G27 has 'combing' marks on the exterior (PRN 156, context 494, not illustrated), and is very similar to other combed sherds on the site, for example context 690 (G14).

Conclusion

The pottery from Downlands can be characterised by a wide range of jars and bowls. No surviving vessel profiles remain and it has not been possible therefore to calculate and compare vessel capacity. Bowls tend to dominate the assemblage, and as burnishing is very labour intensive it suggests that the people living at Downlands required vessels with less permeable surfaces. The increase in bowl forms might be linked with the rise of a particular social activity, namely, eating and drinking (Longley 1980, 73). A wide range of vessel sizes is evident, suitable for preparing, serving and storing food. However, the lack of visible use-wear evidence, for example sooting and burnt residues is a surprising feature of the assemblage. Sooting is the only type of use-wear present, and this appears on just twenty-five sherds (1.3 per cent), including a type R9 vessel (Fig 32, No 16), found in pit 836. It is possible that post depositional processes eroded any use-wear, or that cooking activities were carried out somewhere else, and with different vessels. The pottery may have been used for serving or storing food.

The character of the pottery suggests a population reliant on exploiting available local resources to produce pottery for household use. Ceramic production within Bronze Age and early Iron Age Kent suggests that household level production is taking place, and that each household makes the pottery it requires for its own consumption (Sinopoli 1991, 99; Peacock 1982, 8). However, a small number of vessels have been made with glauconitic sandy clays. The Gault clays from Folkestone are a possible source, and would indicate that potters were travelling some distance to obtain this clay, or that the pots were imported from other settlement sites within the Kent area. This may suggest the emergence of small scale specialised pottery production and distribution.

The pottery derived mostly from pits, and it has been suggested that some of the pits were quarried for potting materials (Jarman 2006, 9). This may well be the case, and a lot of materials would have been needed for pottery manufacture: in particular the rusticated vessels. The rusticated vessels are similar to those from other Kentish sites and it is tentatively suggested that the Downlands potters may have supplied a few other sites with these unusual vessels. A distribution map of rusticated pottery (Macpherson-Grant 1992, 291, fig 7) indicates that potters at Downlands would have been strategically placed both to supply pots to a wider area and to share skills and ideas with potters further afield.

The low average sherd weight and worn surfaces of some of the pottery would imply that these sherds derived from a rubbish collection, which was open to erosion, and subsequently disposed of in pits. Pottery from some of the pits suggests a related group of material; it is possible that the dumping of rubbish may have taken place within quite a short space of time and derived from the same rubbish dump. Placing certain forms within a chronological parameter can be problematic due to their longevity and Downlands bears further evidence to this. Fortunately the assemblage has a range of diagnostic pottery, and implies that the earliest phase of activity began some time in the late Bronze Age decorated phase (800–600 BC) and continued through to the early to middle Iron Age (600 to approximately 350 BC). The presence of rusticated pottery found with red-finished vessels suggests a distinctive cultural package dating to around 500–350 BC (Macpherson-Grant 1992) and is paralleled at other sites in Kent.

The Romano-British pottery
Andrew Savage

Introduction

In total 614 sherds of pottery, weighing *c* 6,223g, were recovered, comprising a wide range of both coarse and fine types. Most of the material dates between the first and mid third century AD. Almost half of this represents 'Belgic' fabric types, although none of these necessarily represent pre-conquest activity. Many of the datable features on the site yielded pottery of probably early Roman date, although most of the quantitatively significant groups represent mid Roman activity. Only a handful of sherds belong to the late third century or later.

The condition of the pottery is generally poor. Sherd sizes tend to be small and there are few useful rim-body profiles. In addition, much of the material has been heavily weathered, and many sherds have lost much of their original surfaces. Of the fifty-four contexts which produced pottery, thirty-seven yielded no more than five sherds, and only nine yielded ten sherds or more. Many of these deposits were physically severely truncated and stratigraphically isolated, and the largest groups, representing mid to late Roman soil horizons and occupation (G24, G25 and G27), appear to consist of redeposited material. Although the limitations of the material preclude detailed statistical interpretation, some useful observations can nonetheless be made, particularly concerning its range and dating.

Methodology

Following the pattern established by Canterbury Archaeological Trust for the analysis of Romano-British pottery from excavations in Canterbury, all of the pottery from the site was examined by eye and with a x20 hand-lens and divided into fabrics using the guidelines established by Peacock (1977) and Orton (1977). The fabrics in each layer were quantified by sherd count and weight. A list of the quantified fabrics is presented in Table 6. Few detailed fabric descriptions are given in this report: instead references are made to descriptions published elsewhere where appropriate.

In this report fabrics are usually referred to by the codes used in the Canterbury Archaeological Trust reference collection, thus: B, 'Belgic'; B/ER, 'Belgic'/early Roman; R, Roman; LR, late Roman. Black-burnished wares 1 and 2 are abbreviated to BB1 and BB2 (fabrics R13 and 14). For ease of use, common names are also used in the summary and the discussion of pottery supply.

Given the generally poor quality of the material, it was decided that the few larger rim sherds which might otherwise be drawn can adequately be described by reference to published parallels or by description, using terms in common usage. Both black-burnished wares and fine Upchurch-type wares are described using the typology established by Monaghan in his study of the pottery of the Upchurch and Thameside pottery industries (Monaghan 1987).

Taphonomy

As stated above, most of the pottery recovered from the site was in poor physical condition, suggesting that very little of it represents primary deposition. Although generally true, it is especially noticeable in all deposits in G24 and G25, soil layers, and G26, a post deposit, all associated with the construction of the aisled building. The condition of this material, and its otherwise heterogeneous nature strongly

Fabric	Number	Weight (g)
B1	2	5
B2	193	2047
B3	1	9
B8	65	506
B9	5	55
B21.2	1	11
BER12	1	3
BER16	3	6
R1	75	839
R5	5	23
R9.1	3	32
R9.2	3	11
R13	6	74
R14	28	295
R14.1	2	21
R16	49	376
R17.1	3	29
R17.2	5	59
R17.3	4	13
R18.2	2	15
R35	1	2
R42	13	137
R43	4	22
R46	5	81
R50	7	602
R71	5	47
R73	20	134
R74	79	448
R98	6	156
R99	2	40
R109	1	1
LR1	3	27
LR2.3	7	77
EMS1	3	11
EMS4	2	9
Total	614	6223

Table 6. Quantified fabrics.

supports the suggestion, that G24 and G25 represent a levelling horizon of redeposited material associated with the construction of the building. The only fresh-looking sherds in these groups were single, small sherds of LR1 and EMS1 (see below). These are much later in date than the other pottery, and probably represent intrusion, either from the truncation of superior deposits, or from elsewhere in the vicinity. Ditch G27, also associated with the building, similarly produced two relatively fresh sherds of LR1 and EMS4, which are likely to be intrusive.

The only deposits on the site which, as a group, yielded pottery in distinctly and consistently fresh-looking condition were the pits (G21) cutting the reworked soil (G14) (see below). Unfortunately the twenty-three pits produced a total of only fourteen small sherds of 'Belgic' or Roman pottery, in addition to larger quantities of prehistoric material.

56

The pottery fabrics

Most of the pottery fabrics are either common in east Kent, or have a more widespread distribution and have therefore been previously discussed and described. No fabric descriptions are given, here, for these wares; instead, references are given, where appropriate, to published descriptions or discussions; they are limited to those considered by the present writer to be reasonably accessible and most relevant, in an east Kent context. In many cases the reference(s) chosen will act as links to further, more extensive bibliographies.

Attention has been drawn to the difficulties in distinguishing between unprovenanced, reduced quartz sand-tempered fabrics in east Kent by Pollard (1995a). They have been divided here simply on the basis of the coarseness of the quartz inclusions.

'Belgic'

B1: grog-tempered ware (fine) (Thompson 1982; Pollard 1995a).
B2: grog-tempered ware (coarse) (Thompson 1982; Pollard 1995a, Tomber and Dore 1998).
B8: sand-tempered ware (coarse) (Pollard 1995a).
B9: sand-tempered ware (fine) (Pollard 1995a).

'Belgic'/early Roman

B/ER16: 'Thanet Dry', silty/sandware (fine/coarse).
Colour: mid or dark grey.
Feel: soft and smooth where burnished, otherwise slightly rough.
Inclusions: sparse, fine, sub-angular clear and colourless quartz set in a fine silty matrix; sparse to moderate fine white mica; occasional rounded ferruginous grains, up to *c* 1mm in diameter; burnt-out organic inclusions, fine to very coarse grains of ?siltstone up to *c* 1.5mm.
Surface treatment: irregular horizontal facet-burnish on exterior and top of rim.
Manufacture: hand-made.
Fracture: finely irregular.

Roman

R1: hard-fired, grog-tempered 'Native Coarse Ware' (Pollard 1995a).
R1.2: grog-tempered ware, transitional between B2 and R1 (Pollard 1995a).
R5: reduced Canterbury sandyware (coarse) (Pollard 1995a).
R9.1: oxidised (pink-buff) Canterbury sandyware (coarse) (Pollard 1995a).
R9.2: oxidised (pink-buff) Canterbury sandyware (fine) (Pollard 1995a)
R13: Dorset black-burnished ware, fabric 1 (BB1) (Tomber and Dore 1998)

R14: black-burnished ware, fabric 2 (BB2), mostly of north Kent (Cooling and Cliffe) manufacture (Monaghan 1987; Tomber and Dore 1998).
R14.1: unslipped reduced sandyware (coarse) in the black-burnished tradition (Pollard 1988; 1995a).
R16: fine Upchurch-type ware (reduced) (Tomber and Dore 1998; see Monaghan 1987, for discussion of all fine Upchurch-types).
R17.1: fine Upchurch-type ware (orange).
R17.2: fine Upchurch-type ware (red).
R17.3: fine Upchurch-type ware (buff).
R18.2: fine Upchurch-type ware (purple-grey, ?unslipped)
R32.1: north Gaulish or Colchester colour-coated ware (Tomber and Dore 1998).
R33: Colchester colour-coated ware (Tomber and Dore 1998).
R35: central Gaulish/Rhenish colour-coated ware (Tomber and Dore 1998).
R37: central Gaulish colour-coated ware (white-cream fabric) (Tomber and Dore 1998).
R42: south Gaulish samian (Webster 1993; Tomber and Dore 1998).
R43: central Gaulish samian (Webster 1993; Tomber and Dore 1998).
R46: east Gaulish samian (Webster 1993; Tomber and Dore 1998).
R50: south Spanish Dressel 20 amphora, Peacock and Williams class 25 (Peacock and Williams 1986; Tomber and Dore 1998).
R71: miscellaneous pink-buff fabrics (Pollard 1995a).
R73: miscellaneous reduced sand-tempered ware (coarse) (Pollard 1995a).
R73.1: reduced sand-tempered ware (coarse), unburnished, but otherwise reflecting the black-burnished tradition (Pollard 1995a).
R74.1: miscellaneous oxidised (orange) sand-tempered ware (coarse); distinguished from R73 on the basis of colour.
R74.2: miscellaneous oxidised (red) sand-tempered ware (coarse); distinguished from R73 on the basis of colour.
R74.3: miscellaneous oxidised (buff) sand-tempered ware (coarse); distinguished from R73 on the basis of colour.
R98: miscellaneous amphorae; unidentified.
R99: miscellaneous mortaria; unidentified.
R109: 'other coarse ware'; unidentified sherds, of mixed temper, difficult to place in a recognized category.

Late Roman

LR1: late Roman grog-tempered ware (coarse) (Pollard 1995b)
LR2.2: ?local reduced, 'over-fired' sand-tempered ware (fine); variant of LR2
LR2.3: ?local reduced sand-tempered ware (coarse) variant of LR2

Pottery supply

In general, the range of forms and fabrics seen falls into the pattern described for the east Kent ceramic 'style zone' by Pollard (1988). Most of the coarse pottery represents types of grog-tempered and sand-tempered coarsewares which are widely distributed within that area, the most significant of these, quantitatively, being B2, B8, R1, R14, R73 and R74. Attention has been drawn to the difficulties in distinguishing between unprovenanced, quartz sand-tempered fabrics in east Kent, by Pollard (1995b), and there is nothing in the character of the Downlands material to suggest a specific source. The site would seem to have received little of its pottery from the Canterbury industry. Although both reduced and oxidised sherds from that source were identified (R5 and R9), they constitute, together, only 1.8 per cent of the assemblage by sherd count and 1.1 per cent by weight. Imported coarsewares are limited to a few sherds of south Spanish Dressel 20, the commonest imported amphora, which is widely found on urban and rural sites of all types.

The range of finewares present is not wide. The most abundant are fine Upchurch-types, R16, R17.1, R17.2, R17.3 and R18.2, which together constitute 10.3 per cent of the pottery by sherd count, 7.9 per cent by weight. The reduced variant R16 is, as generally found elsewhere, by far the most abundant of these.

Samian wares, R42, R43 and R46, constitute 3.6 per cent of the pottery by sherd count, 3.8 per cent by weight. Only two other imported fineware fabrics were recovered, both of Gaulish origin: *terra nigra* (B/ER12) and Central Gaulish/Rhenish colour-coated ware (R35).

Although the limited range and small quantities of imported coarse and fine pottery recovered cannot be used to suggest the presence of high-status occupation on or adjacent to the site, they cannot, in such a small sample, preclude it.

Similarly, it is difficult, given the quantity and quality of the material, to accurately identify and interpret the functionality of the pottery supplied to the site. The subjective impression gained by the writer in this respect, is that the assemblage appears to represent a fairly typical domestic assemblage which has no outstanding characteristics.

Mid first to mid third century

Although 271 sherds, weighing c 595g, have been identified as representing 'Belgic' fabric types principally comprising coarse grog-tempered and sand-tempered wares (B2 and B8), there are no indications, among this material, of definite pre-conquest manufacture. Fabric B8 is thought to date to the period c AD 25–75 in east Kent (Pollard 1988), and it might therefore, suggest activity here in the decades immediately following the conquest, perhaps c AD 50–75. A single sherd of imported early Gaulish *terra nigra* (BER12) representing a platter of form CAM16 (Hawkes and Hull 1947) probably also dates to this period (Rigby 1977). The suite of vessel types represented in B2 is largely restricted to

plain (occasionally comb-decorated) everted-rim storage jars which are commonly found in later first- to second-century deposits in east Kent.

Most of the remainder of the pottery recovered would appear to belong to the late first to second/early third century AD. The principal non-local imports found at Downlands comprise Upchurch-type reduced and oxidised finewares (R16-18) and black-burnished ware (BB2, R14), from north and west Kent. Canterbury reduced and oxidised sandywares, produced in the later first to second centuries, comprise a negligible proportion of the assemblage.

Fineware fabrics, taken together, comprise approximately 14 per cent of the total assemblage by sherd count, 11.7 per cent by weight. The Upchurch area was clearly the most important source of fine pottery, providing c 72 per cent of the fine pottery by sherd count, 66.3 per cent by weight. The commonest forms were beakers and bowls. Samian (R42-46) was the only other significant imported fineware, comprising 25.3 per cent of the fine pottery by sherd count, 33 per cent by weight. It was represented almost exclusively by southern and central Gaulish types (R42 and 43); more than half of the twenty-two sherds of samian are of mid to late first-century southern Gaulish type, R42. Perhaps the most interesting find was that of a single sherd of early Gaulish *terra nigra*. This fabric, which was imported from the late Augustan to early post-conquest period is a relatively uncommon find, and is still principally restricted to urban and higher status rural sites.

BB2 (R14) constituted an important component of pottery assemblages in the mid to late second/early third century in east Kent. As at Canterbury, jars here are under-represented in BB2, when compared with some other sites (Pollard 1988; 1995b), most of these being made in sand- or grog-tempered ware.

Hard-fired grog-tempered ware (R1), was the commonest later Roman coarseware fabric at Downlands in the second/early third century; it was widespread and abundant in east Kent at that time. At Downlands, as elsewhere, this fabric was used almost exclusively to make jars and only occasionally dishes, thus neatly complementing the open forms manufactured in BB2. There were also significant quantities of coarse 'Belgic' grog-tempered ware (B2), almost all of which is likely to be late first to second century in date. Given the usual preponderance of reduced coarseware fabrics in Romano-British pottery assemblages, it is interesting that, among the wheel-thrown sand-tempered wares, seventy-nine sherds of oxidised R74 has been recorded, as opposed to only twenty sherds of reduced R73. This finding is mirrored in the B2 (and indeed in some other fabrics), where a striking and unexpected preponderance of sherds with a reddish appearance is also found. Given that there are no obvious signs of re-firing, and the high degree of weathering observed on many sherds, it is suggested that soil conditions, as well as mechanical wear, may have affected the appearance of a significant part of the assemblage. Although, in theory, it might be argued that such high proportions of oxidised pottery could represent a local production tradition, it is significant that even quantities of pottery such as black-burnished ware (BB2, R14) that, on the basis of form and other fabric characteristics, are clearly not local, have an oxidised appearance. All of the small quantities of late Roman grog-tempered pottery (LR1) and the Anglo-Saxon EMS4 recovered (*see* below) are in distinctly fresh condition when compared to the bulk of the Romano-British pottery from this site, which was redeposited, even when found in association with these earlier, weathered sherds.

The only identified imported coarsewares were twelve sherds (756g) of amphorae. Six of these, (*c* 602g), represent south Spanish Dressel 20 amphorae (Peacock and Williams (1986) class 25, R50). Dressel 20, which carried olive oil, often forms the sole component of amphora assemblages in small settlements and on rural sites, whereas a greater abundance and range of vessel types is found on higher status sites. It accounted for *c* 64 per cent of amphorae from various sites at Canterbury examined by Arthur (1986). The six other 'amphorae' sherds may represent large flagons, and may have been made in east Kent.

Three sherds (*c* 55g) of mortaria were recovered, representing two identified fabrics. One of these, (R61, Hartley fabric 2) was probably made in Kent, possibly at Canterbury (Hartley 1982); the other (R9.2) was certainly made at Canterbury.

Mid third to fourth/early fifth century

Only six sherds, representing R14 bead-and-flange rim dishes and LR1 jars, necessarily belong to the mid third century or later, although it is quite likely that some otherwise undiagnostic sherds of R1, R14, R73, R74, and LR2 may also do so. LR1 dates from the late third to the early fifth century, and was the pre-eminent coarseware from the mid fourth century onwards. In addition, some sherds of R1, R73 and LR2, whose inception lies in the second century, but which continued to be manufactured until at least the late third, may also belong to this period. The small quantities of clearly late coarsewares found, and a total absence of late Roman finewares, suggest, however, that amounts of such material are not likely to be significant. The middle Roman soil horizon, G25, and ditch G27, yielded a few probably intrusive sherds of Anglo-Saxon date.

It should be noted that five sherds (*c* 20g) of early to mid Anglo-Saxon pottery (EMS1 and EMS4) were recovered from contexts otherwise described as Roman (*see* discussion, below).

Dating of the principal features

Early Romano-British occupation

The north boundary of the early Roman occupation (G15 and G16)

The pottery from ditch G15 was entirely prehistoric. The primary fills (255 and 289) of ditch G16 contained a little

ceramic dating evidence. In addition to five sherds of B2, each context yielded a single sherd of R16. The fragment from 289 appears to be from a carinated beaker of Monaghan Class H, which is dated *c* AD 70–130.

Five sherds of Romano-British pottery were recovered from deposits associated with the recutting of ditch, G16. Four sherds of R42, representing the base of a bowl, and probably belonging to the second half of the first century, were recovered from 287 and one sherd of R98/9.2, of probable late first- to second-century date, came from 253 (probably the same vessel as 496, ditch G18, below).

Gullies predating modification of boundary ditch (G17)

Pottery was recovered only from fill 703 of gully 704: two sherds R50, and five of grog-tempered ware classified as R1 (mid to late second or third century). These sherds might, however, represent exceptionally hard-fired B2 and constitute unreliable dating evidence.

Modification of the Romano-British boundary (G18)

The deposits associated with the remodelling of the boundary formed by ditches G15 and G16 yielded little ceramic evidence. There were only twelve sherds and they can only be broadly dated as belonging to the late first or second century. A single sherd was tentatively identified as possible R1, which could be later, but see comments for G17, above.

Horse burial (G20)

There was no pottery directly associated with the horse burial. It was cut by pit 589 whose sole surviving fill (588) yielded thirty-nine sherds of B8, apparently from the same vessel, a pedestal-foot closed form, which is presumably of mid first-century AD date (but see stratigraphic discussion p 41).

Pits cutting reworked pre-Roman soils G14 (G21)

There were twenty-one such pits, which were mostly aceramic. Fourteen sherds were recovered, from six of the pits. The relatively fresh condition of this material has been discussed above. Although any dating based on such small samples can only be considered highly speculative, contexts 475, 516, and 572 produced only B2 and B9, suggesting a mid first-century date, whilst B2 and R16 from 667 may indicate the late first to second century. Tiny scraps of R16 and R74 from 675 and 730 can only be dated broadly to the late first to third and later first to fourth century, respectively.

Mid Romano-British soil horizon

G24 levelling/colluviation outside building.

Eighty-one sherds (*c* 1,519g) were recovered, all from soil horizon (481). Although the assemblage included residual first-century material (forty-one sherds of B2, nine sherds of B8 and one sherd from an R42 platter base), it includes material which is clearly of at least early to mid second-century or later date. There were six sherds of R14, including a simple-rim dog-dish and a roll-rim pie-dish with burnished linear decoration, cf Monaghan Class 4. Coarsewares include both reduced and oxidised sand-tempered wares (R73, 74), and grog-tempered ware (B2, R1). Forms in these fabrics were restricted to typologically undiagnostic everted rim fragments.

There were two sherds of a single central Gaulish samian platter, probably a Drag 18–31, likely to date c AD 120–80.

There was also a single rim sherd of R50 typologically resembling Martin-Kilcher type 24 (1983), as presented in Peacock and Williams (1986) which is dated to the early second century. The present example may be of similar date, or perhaps later.

The poor condition of this pottery has been noted above. Although no cross-joins were noted between individual vessels in G24 and those in G25 and G26, also associated with the building (see below), the pottery from these deposits is so generally homogeneous and similar in condition that it may well represent redeposition from one source.

Mid to late Romano-British occupation

Possible terrace for construction of building (G25)

In total, 163 sherds (c 1,417g) were recovered, most (115 sherds) coming from layer 239, inside the walls of the building. The remaining thirty-seven sherds came from levelling horizons 234, 235, and 236.

The pottery from 239 has a generally uniform murky orange-brown appearance (*see* p 58). Thirty-nine sherds were classified as R1, and although some of these sherds might represent exceptionally hard-fired B2, others were more certain identifications.

Among the nineteen sherds identified as R73 or 74, there were three rim sherds which may be compared to forms common in LR2 (Pollard 1995b, 727, fig 314, no 490). Among six sherds of R14 there were four rims; three of these represent rounded roll-rim pie-dishes. The fourth, although damaged, clearly represents a dish of bead-and-flange-rim type, dating to the mid third century or later. As is the case with fill 285 of ditch 286, G27, however, the context also yielded single sherds of LR1 and EMS1.

The character of the albeit small quantity of pottery from 234, 235 and 236, though lacking the LR and EMS wares, is otherwise similar in character to that from 239, within the building. Sherds from an R46 Drag 36 dish, probably the same vessel, were recovered from each context. It is likely to be late second to mid third century in date.

Aisled building (G26)

Only one of the aisle-post deposits associated with the Roman building, 245, produced pottery There were sixteen

sherds, weighing 22g, of broadly similar character to those recovered from the deposits filling the terrace, G25 (*see* above). One fragment of an R13 dish is probably part of the same vessel as a sherd from 239.

L-shaped ditch associated with building (G16)

Fifty-nine sherds (c 691g) were recovered, approximately 90 per cent coming from fill 285. This group bears close comparison with that recovered from mid Roman soil horizon, G24. Although it includes a somewhat smaller proportion of coarse sandywares than the former (27 per cent, by sherd count, as opposed to 38 per cent, a difference which, given the sample size may not be significant), it is in other respects strikingly similar in both composition and date. The only fabrics present which were not also identified in G24 are a single sherd from an R35 folded beaker, probably dating c AD 150–200, and five sherds of LR2.3, a fabric which is contemporary with R1. The latter included two typical everted rim sherds, cf Pollard 1995b (720, fig 309, no 380). There were nine sherds of R14, which included a bead-and-flange rim fragment, cf Monaghan Class 4, which is likely to date to the mid third century or later. It is tempting, on the basis of this vessel, to date the deposit as being at least as late as the mid third century; this would be consistent with the presence of R1 and LR2.3 which dates from the later second century until at least the end of the third. That the piece is intrusive however, cannot be precluded as the context also yielded single sherds of LR1 and EMS4 even though the sherd in question lacks the fresh appearance of the latter.

Pottery from fill 397 included sherds of an R9.2 flagon, probably dating c AD 70–200. A single sherd from an R14 chamfered-base dish, dating later than c AD 120, was recovered from (494).

Other deposits

No other individually significant groups were recovered. The small quantities of pottery recovered from individual features are in general consistent with the material described above. Many features are likely to be of 'Belgic'/early Roman date, yielding little other than a few sherds of B2 and B8, occasionally accompanied by R42.

The lithic assemblage

Lynne Bevan (with a contribution by Robert Hosfield)

Introduction

The assemblage comprised 173 items of worked flint weighing in total c 3,000g. Table 7 illustrates the artefactual breakdown of the assemblage, the majority of which came from prehistoric features. The material was examined, classified, and catalogued, with the aid of a hand lens at x10 magnification. The individual weight and identification of all items was recorded and this information is held with the site archive.

Due to the limited and largely residual nature of the finds, selection for illustration was restricted to the three most chronologically diagnostic or otherwise significant items in the assemblage (Fig 36, Nos 1–4). For clarity, non-illustrated material is referred to by individual find/context number.

Core/core fragments	6/5
Flakes and chunks	142
Hammerstone	1
Scrapers	6
Other retouched	13

Table 7. Artefactual breakdown of assemblage.

Raw material

The raw material used for the production of the flint assemblage mainly comprised flint pebbles of a generally unpredictable quality. When present, remnant cortex was thin and compacted and characteristic of pebble flint from secondary deposits, the most probable source being local beach pebbles. A quantity of large unworked beach pebbles was discarded during the sorting and identification process but the worked flint, which was probably derived from the same source, was found to be in a generally good condition, almost exclusively glossy and fresh, with very little abrasion noted. Several flints with internal voids and crystalline inclusions were noted among the artefacts, resulting in a high incidence of hinge fractures. Flint colours ranged from light grey and light brown to medium and darker brown and grey, with the majority of pieces being translucent rather than opaque. There was a very low incidence of white recortication (resulting from chemical changes in the soil) and no burning noted among the struck flint.

An exhausted flake core (FN 289) and a flake core fragment (FN 317), weighing 140g and 47g respectively, were of a distinctive dark brown flint with an orange stripe under the cortex. This flint is reminiscent of flint from the Bullhead Beds which is found on many sites in the London area and occurs naturally in the Thames terrace gravels, and is usually sourced to the Thanet Sand over Chalk (Cotton 2002, 69). This kind of flint, or a similarly distinctive flint, may have been imported to the site from some distance away.

Discussion and dating

The earliest item in the assemblage was a Palaeolithic flake tool (Fig 36, No 1), possibly a convergent scraper of earlier Palaeolithic date, that is Lower to Middle Palaeolithic rather than Upper Palaeolithic (Robert Hosfield, pers comm). However, the identification and dating of this item was hampered by its heavy patination and edge-damage.

None of the other flints in the collection were closely datable and the earliest among them may be a retouched flake/

fabricator with small, narrow blade detachments on its dorsal (Fig 36, No 2), which may date to the later Mesolithic–early Neolithic period. This item would appear to be a residual find in a middle Roman feature (context 481). Two blade core fragments from contexts 690 and 914 (Fig 36, No 3 and FN 323 respectively), the latter from a prehistoric feature (context 914), might be of later Neolithic date and thus earlier than the majority of the flint assemblage. The remainder of the cores and core fragments exhibited flake detachments and were probably of Bronze Age to Iron Age date, in common with the majority of flakes, which tended to be broad and squat. Such flakes, as opposed to narrow blade-like flakes, are usually the product of poor flint-knapping techniques, characterised by an absence of formal platform preparation. They are generally associated with later prehistoric industries dating to the later Neolithic to Bronze Age (eg Pitts 1978), although they may also date to the Iron Age, according to recent research (Young and Humphrey 1999; Humphrey and Young 2003).

Only one of the scrapers, a large ovoid side and end form (Fig 36, No 4), had been finely worked. Typologically this item would not look out of place in a later Neolithic context, in common with one of the blade core fragments (Fig 36, No 3), discussed above, which came from the same context, along with seven flakes (context 690). This debitage, which was all in a fresh condition and appeared to come from the same nodule, perhaps represents a primary knapping episode. However, the later phasing of this context, which has been dated to the late Iron Age–early Roman period, would tend to argue against this, since it is generally accepted that flintworking did not continue into the Roman period (eg Butler 2005, 191). Conversely, although late Iron Age/early Roman flintworking has not been conclusively identified elsewhere, apart from perhaps at Kimmeridge, Dorset in connection with the shale industry (Sunter and Woodward 1987), it is not entirely impossible that flint was indeed being worked this late in other locations. Turner and Wymer have suggested that Roman stonemasons would have been quite familiar with the techniques of working both stone and flint (1987, 54–5).

Flint scrapers like the illustrated example from context 690 at Downlands (Fig 36, No 4) may have been used in connection with a particular craft activity such as skin-working. There have been instances in non-western societies of stone tools continuing in use for hide-scraping long after the adoption of iron tools for most other purposes, due to the particularly effective use of stone scrapers for this task (eg Gallagher 1977).

The other scrapers and retouched flakes from Downlands were rough, marginally retouched artefacts, many of which exhibited use-wear, and none of which is datable. However, such a limited range of retouched pieces, which tended to be produced for expedient purposes and immediate use and discard, are typical of later Bronze Age and Iron Age flint assemblages. Later Bronze Age and Iron Age flintworking share a number of characteristics, including a reduced repertoire of identifiable tools. With regard to the middle Bronze Age assemblage from Grimes Graves, Norfolk, Herne suggested that as flint was expected to fulfil fewer functions there was less incentive to invest time in flint procurement and flintworking. Instead the emphasis was on the expedient manufacture of a limited range of flint tools which included scrapers, awls and some knife forms found in settlement contexts and bound up in the domestic mode of production (Herne 1991, 67). A similarly reduced repertoire of identifiable tool types and a number of miscellaneous, barely-modified, retouched pieces was identified in the late Bronze Age assemblage from the riverside zone at Runnymede Bridge, Egham, Surrey (Bevan forthcoming).

The question of flint usage continuing during the Iron Age (Young and Humphrey 1999; Humphrey and Young 2003), rather than ceasing during the late Bronze Age (Saville 1981, 6), should be considered on sites such as Downlands where much of the flint was recovered from Iron Age contexts. However, Iron Age flintworking is very difficult to identify, since few formal tools were produced and there are no specific Iron Age tool types (Young and Humphrey 1999, 233). Nevertheless, some typical characteristics of early to middle Iron Age flint assemblages were present in this small assemblage. These included: small assemblage size, use of poor quality local materials, simple core/flake technology, a restricted range of formal tool types, a predominance of secondary and inner flakes, a low incidence of formal cores and a prevalence of broad squat flakes (Humphrey and Young 2003, 87). At Runnymede Bridge formal flake cores were few in number and there was a high incidence of large struck pieces, the result of a 'smash and grab' technology in which nodules were smashed up in order to produce flakes which could be used for expedient purposes and then discarded. A similarly 'high instance of chips and chunks' has been observed among other late Bronze Age and Iron Age assemblages (Humphrey and Young 2003, 87). There was also a high incidence of hinge fractures among the assemblage from Downlands, which often results from the use of low quality, local flint, and the cores were irregular-shaped, which, again, is also a characteristic of Iron Age flintworking (ibid, 80), when skilled core reduction was not required.

The commonly-held view that the decline in flint use for tool manufacture during the Bronze Age was simply linked to an increasing availability of metal artefacts has been criticised (Humphrey and Young 2003, 79). However, by the middle Bronze Age 'the definition of personal identity and the negotiation of political authority became more intimately associated with the display, circulation and formal deposition of metal artefacts' (Edmonds 1995, 187). As flint lost its importance as a medium for expressing ideas about status, it became regarded as a more utilitarian substance, continuing to be used in the domestic sphere during the middle Bronze Age (Herne 1991, 67; Edmonds 1995, 122–83) and the later Bronze Age (Bevan forthcoming). A similarly domestic context of production is now envisaged for Iron Age flint usage (Humphrey and Young 2003, 84).

During the late Bronze Age and Iron Age, flintworking took place in a domestic context at Downlands for a range of utilitarian purposes, the evidence for which is limited due to the small size of the assemblage and the undiagnostic character of the flint, which mainly comprised unretouched flakes, though two small collections of flint (contexts 800, pit 801 and 588, pit 589), both of which may represent possible primary knapping episodes at the site, have now been dated to the late Bronze Age/early Iron Age. Though undiagnostic in their composition, comprising mainly rough debitage, they lend support for flintworking here during this very late period. While the presence of the cores and waste flakes attests to flintworking on the site, presumably for domestic purposes, based on the current assemblage its exact nature remains enigmatic.

1   Flake tool, possibly a convergent scraper, heavily patinated and edge-damaged. Possibly of earlier Palaeolithic (Lower–Middle) date. Context 496, FN 271. Fig 36, No 1.

2   Retouched flake/fabricator with small, narrow blade detachments on its dorsal, light grey opaque flint. Possibly later Mesolithic–early Neolithic in date. Context 481, FN 153. Fig 36, No 2.

3   Core fragment with broad blade detachments, light grey-brown, speckled, translucent and opaque flint. Possibly later Neolithic in date. Context 690, FN 306a. Length: 40mm, width: 32mm, thickness: 10mm. Fig 36, No 3.

4   Ovoid side and end scraper, light brown translucent flint, with extensive retouch around 70 per cent of its circumference. Typologically later Neolithic in date. Length: 60 mm, width: 45mm, thickness: 13mm. Context 690, FN 306b. Fig 36, No 4.

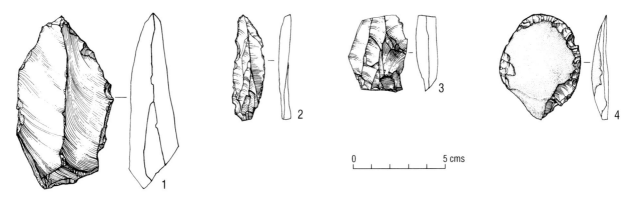

0 _____ 5 cms

Fig 36. 1: Palaeolithic ?scraper; 2: retouched flake or fabricator; 3: blade core fragment; 4: ovoid scraper. Scale 1:2.

The small finds

Lynne Bevan

Introduction

Eighteen numbered and registered 'small finds' (excluding iron nails and fragments of slag) comprising sixteen individual objects, were recovered from the site. The earliest are Iron Age in date, though the majority of the assemblage comprises Roman objects. Most are made of either iron or copper alloy. With the exception of a fragment from a fired clay weight dated to the Iron Age and two brooches of Iron Age and Iron Age/early Roman date respectively, none of the objects was sufficiently well-preserved or artefactually interesting or unusual to warrant illustration. A descriptive catalogue of all diagnostic items is provided below and a listing by context of all nails and slag fragments is held with the site archive.

The finds will be considered below, first by material of manufacture, given that the relatively small size of the assemblage precludes the kind of functional grouping of objects favoured by most Roman small finds specialists today, following the lead of Nina Crummy's analysis of material from excavations in Colchester in the 1970s (Crummy 1983).

Objects of fired clay

The only small find of fired clay was a fragment from a triangular Iron Age weight which had retained a pierced corner and thus probably conforms to Poole type 1 based upon the morphology of Iron Age weights from Danebury (Poole 1991, 406). This weight came from a prehistoric feature (context 850, FN 263) and, like similar weights from Danebury and other Iron Age sites, was probably originally used suspended from a loom. Two other fired clay fragments were recovered, weighing 9 and 13g respectively (contexts 579 and 845, not illustrated).

1   Fragment from a triangular Iron Age weight probably of Poole type 1 (Poole 1984, 406). This was probably a loomweight. Width of only surviving complete face: 500mm, diameter of pierced hole: 13mm, weight: 171g. Context 850, FN 263. Prehistoric. Fig 37, No 1.

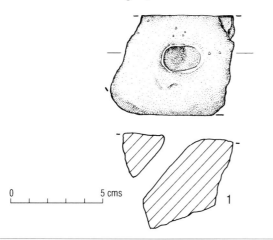

Fig 37. Weight fragment. Scale 1:2.

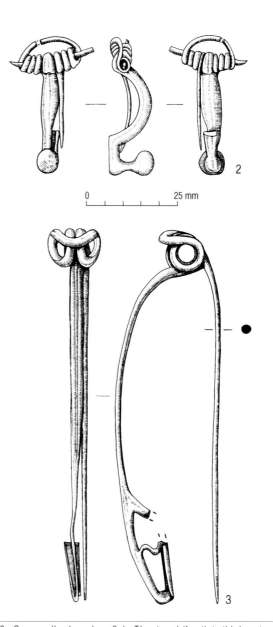

Fig 38. Copper alloy brooches. 2: La Tène type I (fourth to third century BC); 3: La Tène type III (first century BC/AD). Scale 1:1.

Objects of copper alloy

Objects of copper alloy were well preserved and included two brooches. The earliest brooch (Fig 38, No 2) was a La Tène type I brooch dating to the fourth to third century BC (Hattatt 1989, fig 147.220, 724, 288), a close parallel for which was recovered from Cold Kitchen Hill in Wiltshire (*ibid*, fig 147.220). The second brooch (Fig 38, No 3) was a large, complete La Tène type III brooch dated to the first century BC/AD (*ibid*, fig 149.290), with an elaborate coiled spring, an openwork catch-plate and linear decoration on its narrow bow. The closest parallels for this brooch come from Ipswich, Suffolk (*ibid*, fig 149.8, 290) and France, the latter being described as 'Nauheim type progenitors' (*ibid*, fig 149.734, 735, 290). The stylistic dating of both of these brooches is entirely in keeping with the dating of their contexts at Downlands.

63

Other copper alloy finds consisted of a hollow tube-shaped fitting or ferrule (No 4, not illustrated), a round-sectioned ring, probably a clothes fitting (No 5, not illustrated), a possible nail or stud head (No 6, not illustrated), and three unidentified fragments (Nos 7–9, not illustrated).

2 Copper alloy La Tène type I brooch, almost complete, with pin intact but some damage to the catch-plate, dating to the fourth to third century BC. Length: 38mm. Width of spring end: 24mm. Context 835, FN 329. Prehistoric. Fig 38, No 2.

3 Copper alloy La Tène type III brooch dated to the first century BC/AD, complete, with an elaborate coiled spring, an openwork catch-plate and linear decoration on its narrow bow. It is now slightly bent out of shape, probably the result of post-depositional processes. Length: 100mm. Width (closed) at centre: 22mm. Context 516, FN 325. Late Iron Age/early Roman. Fig 38, No 3.

4 A hollow tapering copper alloy tube in two fragments. Probably a small fitting or ferrule. Length: 23mm, diameter: 3mm, tapering to 1mm. Context 561, FN 326. Prehistoric. Not illustrated.

5 A small, undecorated, round-sectioned copper alloy ring. Probably a clothes fitting. Diameter: 10mm, thickness: 1mm. Context 364, FN 148. Modern context. Not illustrated.

6 Small, round-sectioned piece of copper alloy, possibly the head of a stud or a nail. Diameter: 4mm. Context 342, FN 145. Late Iron Age/early Roman. Not illustrated.

7 Small, undiagnostic fragment of copper alloy plate, roughly square in shape. Dimensions: 7mm x 6mm, thickness: 2mm. Context 363, FN 147. Prehistoric. Not illustrated.

8 Roughly crescent-shaped piece of copper alloy, possibly originally part of a fitting, but too corroded and fragmentary to otherwise identify. Length: 15mm, width: 8mm, thickness: 4mm. Context 723, FN 327. Prehistoric. Not illustrated.

9 Roughly triangular-shaped piece of folded copper alloy sheet, probably scrap metal for melting and re-use. Length: 23mm. Width: 14mm tapering to 3mm. Context 328, FN 835. Prehistoric. Not illustrated.

Iron objects

Iron objects were few in number and poorly-preserved, with a high incidence of corrosion. For this reason none has been illustrated. Almost all of them came from contexts dated to the middle Roman period. They comprised a spatulate-headed linch pin (No 10), a fragmentary joiner's dog (No 11), a fragment of blade from a tool or knife (No 12), a curved fragment of strip or band (No 13) and eighteen iron nails.

The linch pin (No 10) conforms to Manning's Type 2b linch pin, the most common Roman type, many examples of which have been found on sites in Britain and Germany (Manning 1985, fig 20:2b, 72-72, plate 31:H42). The joiner's dog (No 11) was in a worse state of preservation,

in three fragments, with one arm broken off. This common type of Roman object was used for joining timbers together (*ibid*, plate 61:R52, 131). The other finds were too small for more than a broad identification as Roman ironwork. The nails were, again, very corroded and most were fragmentary. Of some interest in the collection were four hobnails from Roman footwear (two from context 239 and two from context 502). These small distinctive nails conform with Manning's Type 10 nails often associated with burials (*ibid*, fig 32.10, 133, 136), although they are equally likely to have survived in refuse contexts as the remains of discarded, worn-out shoes. The other nails were too corroded and fragmentary to relate to Manning's nail typology but it seems likely that they conformed to the most common types 1a and 1b (*ibid*, fig 32.1a and 1b, 132) which would have been used for general building purposes. One of the nails was found in close association with the joiner's dog (No 11), and two other nails came from the same context (486, FN 255).

10 Complete spatulate-headed linch pin, the head of which is probably formed by a turned-over loop, which is now obscured by corrosion products. Length: 126mm. Width of head: 51mm. Height of loop: 48mm. Context 239, FN 135. Middle Roman. Not illustrated.

11 Joiner's dog, with one arm broken off, now in three fragments. Length: 115mm. Length of surviving arm: 49mm. Width of upper surface: 24mm. Context 486, FN 324. Middle Roman. Not illustrated.

12 Fragment of blade from a tool or knife. Length: 33mm. Width: 20mm. Context 513, FN 258. Late Iron Age/early Roman. Not illustrated.

13 Curved fragment of iron strip or band. Length: 28mm. Diameter: 11mm. Context 486, FN 256. Middle Roman. Not illustrated.

Objects of worked stone[1]

Items of worked stone comprised a broken sandstone rubbing stone or possible saddle quern (No 14) and four small sandstone fragments from rotary quernstones, three of which were from the same quern (Nos 15–16). The working surface of No 14 was smooth to the touch as the result of heavy usage. The material used for both rotary querns was very similar, with the quern from context 687 (No 17) being of a slightly coarser material than that used for the medium-grained sandstone quern from context 481 (Nos 15–16). Both are probably Millstone Grit.

In addition, a small fragment of Hertfordshire Puddingstone (conglomerate) was identified which had not obviously been worked but may have originated from a third quern, either being a broken or waste fragment (context 659, FN 331). Hertfordshire Puddingstone is a well-known material for quern manufacture (Rob Ixer, pers comm).

---

1 Geological identification by Rob Ixer.

14 Rubbing stone or possible saddle quern, roughly triangular in shape, broken at one corner, with a worn working surface which is smooth to the touch. Medium to coarse-grained, pale coloured, inhomogenous sandstone, with small quartz pebbles up to half a centimetre in diameter. Dimensions: approximately 300 by 190mm and 70mm thick. Context 203, FN 124. Prehistoric. Not illustrated.

15 Two fragments from the same quern, probably from the lower stone of the pair, each with a slightly dished and smoothed upper surface. Pink-brown, well-cemented, micaceous arkosic sandstone, probably Millstone Grit. Dimensions of largest fragment: 148 by 220mm and 56mm thick. Context 481, FN 264. Middle Roman. Not illustrated.

16 Quern fragment with part of outer edge surviving, from the same quern as the other two fragments from this context (No 15). Again, with a heavily worn upper surface. Pink-brown, well-cemented, micaceous arkosic sandstone, probably Millstone Grit. Dimensions: approximately 124 by 105mm and 44mm thick. Context 481, FN 265. Middle Roman. Not illustrated.

17 Quern fragment, with wear marks on surviving upper surface. Coarse grained pale pink feldspathic sandstone, probably Millstone Grit. Dimensions: approximately 80 by 80mm and 56mm thick. Context 687, FN 261. Early Roman. Not illustrated.

Slag

A total weight of 1,818g of smithing slag and 471g of tap or bloomery slag, the latter represented by two pieces only, was recovered from the site.

4
Palaeoenvironmental evidence

The mammal bone
Robin Bendrey

Introduction

The assemblage was retrieved by hand-excavation and bulk sieved samples (Tables 8 and 11). Animal bone was derived from contexts dated to the following periods: prehistoric; early Roman; middle Roman

Mammal bone was recorded following Dobney and Rielly (1988). If it was not possible to identify a fragment to species an animal-size category was awarded, for example cattle-sized, otherwise it was labelled indeterminate. The assemblage has been identified with the aid of a comparative osteological reference collection and a number of publications (Amorosi 1989; Boessneck 1969; Payne 1985; Schmid 1972). As no goat bones were identified in the assemblage the material identified as sheep/goat (Table 8) is considered as sheep in the text. Cattle, sheep and pig mandibular toothwear data have been recorded following Grant (1982). Crown height measurements were recorded from equid teeth following Levine (1982). Measurements have been taken following von den Driesch (1976). The assemblage is quantified by number of fragments (NISP) and context/sample frequency (O'Connor 1985).

The hand-recovered assemblage

Taxonomic representation

Although some 3,000 fragments were recovered from stratified features (Table 8), the majority of these are associated with a horse burial (G20). This skeleton is discussed in detail below. The fragmentation of parts of this skeleton has resulted in a large number of comminuted bone fragments (Table 8). Quantification by number of fragments clearly over-represents the presence of horse on site, due to the skeleton. A less biased picture of taxonomic representation can be achieved by considering the fragmentary assemblage, excluding bones deriving from the horse skeleton, and also by considering context frequency. Context frequency measures the number of contexts in which a taxon occurs, and allows assessment of the occurrence of the species throughout the site independently of its numerical abundance (O'Connor 1985).

The relatively small sample size of the fragmentary bone assemblage (ie excluding the horse skeleton) limits the information available. Little can be made from the quantification data to draw conclusions on the relative abundance of the taxa present. By number of fragments, cattle is the most common taxon recovered from the

period	Prehistoric								Late Iron Age/early Roman							Middle Roman			Total
group	2	3	4	5	7	8	9	Total	14	15	16	18	20	21	Total	25	27	Total	NISP
cattle	4	19	1	2			2	28	1				1	6	8	1	17	18	54
sheep/goat†	9	6	1			1	2	19					1	3	4		2	2	25
(sheep		1			1			2											2)
horse	1	1		1	1			4					155*	1	156		1	1	161
pig														1	1	1	1	2	3
dog																	3	3	3
sheep/goat/roe deer														1	1				1
cattle-sized	6	17		4	3		3	33	1		3		968‡	10	982	2	45	47	1062
sheep-sized		2				1		3				1			1	4	1	5	9
indeterminate		18	2	7	1			28		2			1605‡	22	1629		71	71	1728
Total	20	63	2	9	11	2	8	115	1	3	3	1	2730	44	2782	10	139	149	3046

Table 8. Distribution of mammal bone, by number of identified fragments (NISP). † = sheep/goat includes the specimens identified to sheep; * = complete skeleton; ‡ = mostly fragments from horse skeleton.

prehistoric features, followed by sheep and then horse (Table 8). This rank order is also seen in the context frequency data (Table 9).

Cattle remains are also the most common by number of fragments from the early Roman phase of activity on site (excluding the horse skeleton). The context frequency data indicates that cattle and horse are the most common taxa, followed by sheep (Table 9), although horse is over-represented as the skeleton derived from two contexts from G20. Cattle remains are also the most common by number of fragments and context frequency from the middle Roman phases of activity on site (Tables 8 and 9).

It is likely, that the large-boned taxa, such as cattle and horse, are over-represented relative to the small-boned taxa, such as sheep, pig and dog, due to preservation and recovery factors (see below). In general, the material is too limited to make any inference, as variation in this small assemblage may be associated with intra-site context variability associated with differential disposal and recovery.

Taphonomy

The state of preservation of the animal bone assemblage is generally good. Carnivore gnawing is generally low, being recorded on 2.8 per cent of the fragmentary (disarticulated) bone assemblage (9/320).

Age, sex and size

Age and sex data are very limited. A prehistoric cattle mandible (G3) is aged as 'old adult', following Halstead (1985). A middle Roman (G27) male pig mandible is aged to 7–14 months, following Hambleton (1999). A prehistoric (G2) equid upper third molar is aged to 14–15 years, following Levine (1982).

There is insufficient metrical data to explore the sizes of the animals contributing to the fragmentary assemblage.

Pathology

Two specimens in the fragmentary assemblage exhibit pathological, or sub-pathological, changes. There is a slight depression on the surface of a prehistoric (G8) sheep horn core. This has been associated with malnutrition in some animals (Hatting 1975, 346), but the significance in this one specimen is uncertain.

A prehistoric (G5) horse anterior proximal phalanx exhibits bilateral osteophytosis of the distal abaxial borders in the insertion of the collateral ligaments of the interphalangeal joint (see Rooney 1997), with extension of new bone formation down the sides of the shaft towards the distal end and round onto the anterior side of the diaphysis. The identification of these lesions in the fossil equid record indicates that this is a naturally occurring condition (Rooney 1997), although it may also be work-related. In the absence of an accurate age-at-death for this animal the significance of this pathology is uncertain.

The horse skeleton

An oval pit (G20) dated to the late Iron Age/early Roman period, and measuring 2m by 1.5m and less than 1m deep (see p 34), produced the articulating complete skeleton of a horse (Equus caballus) (Table 10).

Size, age and sex

The presence of full sized canines indicates that the horse was male. The animal stood around 1.174 metres, or 11.2 hands, high at the withers [using the factors of Kiesewalter (1888) to reconstruct the stature]. Selected post-cranial measurements are presented in Table 10. All the vertebrae are fully fused, indicating an age at death in excess of 5 years (Silver 1969). Estimates of age based on cheek tooth crown height measurements ranged from 7–10 years at death, although most fall into the range 7–9 years (Levine 1982). Estimate of age based on incisor wear indicate an age of around 9 years old at death (Cornevin and Lesbre 1894).

Disposition and taphonomy

There is evidence for the breaking of bones in all four limbs at, or soon after, death. The left and right tibia, and the right radius and ulna, have all been broken through the proximal part of the diaphysis. The evidence for the left forelimb is uncertain, but the ulna appears to have been broken at the proximal articulation. The characteristics of these fractures suggest that the bones were broken while fresh (see Outram 2001), and there is no evidence for healing. There is no further evidence for butchery or other evidence for modification to the skeleton. An interpretation would be that the legs were broken to fit the horse into the pit. This is supported by the disposition of the horse within the (relatively small) pit, in that its front legs were folded in and twisted up against the pit's western end (Crispin Jarman, pers comm).

	Prehistoric		Late Iron Age/ early Roman		Middle Roman	
	cf	rf	cf	rf	cf	rf
cattle	11	0.58	3	0.38	3	0.60
sheep/goat	5	0.26	2	0.25	1	0.20
horse	4	0.21	3	0.38	1	0.20
pig			1	0.13	2	0.40
dog					1	0.20
sheep/goat/roe deer			1	0.13		
cattle-sized	8	0.42	6	0.75	3	0.60
sheep-sized	2	0.11	1	0.13	4	0.80
indeterminate	4	0.21	4	0.50	2	0.40
Total	19	1.00	8	1.00	5	1.00

Table 9. Distribution of mammal bone, by context frequency. Context frequency (cf) is a count of the number of contexts that contained a taxon, and the relative frequency (rf) is the number as a proportion of the total number of bone-producing contexts (O'Connor 1985).

element	side	measurement						
		GL	GLC	Bp	SD	Bd		
femur	left		309		33.5			
femur	right				32.9			
		GLP	BG	SLC	LG			
scapula	left	78.7	41.4		48.5			
scapula	right	78.2	40.7	55.6				
		GLl	GLC	SD		BT	HTC	
humerus	left			29.3				
humerus	right		232	30.8		64.2	32.4	
		GL	Ll	Bp	BFp	SD	Bd	BFd
radius	left		274	71.7	64.2	33.5	64.2	54.6
radius	right						64.5	54.5
		GL	Ll	Bp	Dp	SD	Bd	Dd
metacarpal	left	187	180	42.8		29.5	44.6	
metacarpal	right	187	179	43.7	28.6	30.3		
		LA	LAR					
pelvis	left	60.1	52.2					
pelvis	right							
		GL	Ll	Bp	SD	Bd	Dd	
tibia	left				34.1	63.2	41.1	
tibia	right				35.4	62.2	40.8	
		GH	GB	BFd	LMT			
astragalus	left	51	54	44.4	52.7			
astragalus	right	51	53	44.9				
		GL	GB					
calcaneum	left	91.1						
calcaneum	right	90.6	45					
		GL	Ll	Bp	Dp	SD	Bd	Dd
metatarsal	left	229	223	41.4	39.1	26.1	44.5	
metatarsal	right	229	223	42.8	39.5	26.5	45.1	33.3

Table 10. Horse skeleton (G20): selected post-cranial measurements (measurements follow von den Driesch 1976).

Pathology

The left and right anterior proximal phalanges exhibit bilateral osteophytosis of the distal abaxial borders in the insertion of the collateral ligaments of the interphalangeal joints. As discussed above, the identification of these lesions in the fossil equid record indicates that this is a naturally occurring condition (Rooney 1997), but may also be associated with work. There was no evidence for bitting damage on the lower second premolars (following Bendrey 2007b), although this does not mean that the horse was not worked.

Proliferative periosteal lesions are recorded on six rib fragments. These are expressed to a greater extent on the medial side - indicating a pulmonary infection, rather than a penetrating wound. In addition, there are proliferative periosteal lesions on four fragments of vertebrae, three of which can be identified as thoracic vertebrae. One of these also has probable lytic lesions on the lateral surface of the centrum (Plate 9). The evidence for pathology on a number of ribs and vertebrae suggest a systemic infection (although it is a possibility that the pathology noted in the ribs and the vertebrae is associated with separate infections).

Similar pathological manifestations have been described in an Iron Age horse skeleton from Viables Farm, Hampshire (Bendrey 2007a; 2008). In this skeleton proliferative periosteal lesions are also recorded on the medial sides of the ribs and on several of the vertebrae, and lytic destruction is noted in one vertebra. Bendrey (2007a; 2008) argues that these pathologies may represent a systemic infection of tuberculosis or brucellosis. A summary of the interpretation put forward is as follows: the new reactive bone formation on the internal surfaces of the ribs indicates a pulmonary primary infection in the horse; the new reactive bone formation on various vertebrae, from the atlas to the sacrum, and the pelvis indicates the spread of this infection; the resorptive pits in the thoracic vertebra indicate the establishment of the bacteria in this bone. A similar interpretation can be advanced for the Downlands horse.

In the Downlands horse, the rib lesions indicate a pulmonary infection, and the possible identification as either tuberculosis or brucellosis is based on the additional lesions in the vertebrae. In such infections, the bacteria, spread through the circulatory or lymphatic system, tend to lodge in vascular cancellous bone (such as the vertebrae) and can

Plate 9. Right lateral view of thoracic vertebra from the horse skeleton (G 20), showing areas of new woven bone and areas of possible lytic lesions. Scale 1:1.

result in areas of bone destruction to these elements (Baker and Brothwell 1980, 76; Lignereux and Peters 1999, 340–1). Such resorptive pits are also considered as pathological indicators of these diseases in human vertebrae (Aufderheide and Rodríguez-Martín 1998, 140 and 193; Baker 1999, 301). However, it must be remembered that comparative data for the manifestation of these diseases in domestic animals is extremely rare (Lignereux and Peters 1999) and both diseases may produce different manifestations in different species; for example, in dogs the skeletal involvement of tuberculosis results in bone cell proliferation rather than the demineralisation of bone as seen in humans (Bathurst and Barta 2004, 919).

The sieved samples

Consideration of the bones recovered from the bulk sieved samples allows controls to be placed on the data from the hand-recovered assemblage. The most useful material in

group	Prehistoric		Late Iron Age/ early Roman		Middle Roman	
	sf	rf	sf	rf	sf	rf
cattle	4	0.14				
sheep/goat	9	0.32	1	0.17	2	0.33
horse	1	0.04				
pig	1	0.04	1	0.17		
dog	1	0.04	1	0.17		
dog/fox					1	0.17
mole					1	0.17
Total	28	1.00	6	1.00	6	1.00

Table 11. Distribution of mammal bone from sieved samples, by sample frequency. Sample frequency (sf) is a count of the number of samples that contained a taxon, and the relative frequency (rf) is the number as a proportion of the total number of bone-producing samples (O'Connor 1985).

this respect is that from the prehistoric period, as the largest number of bone-producing samples came from this period (Table 11). Sheep/goat is identified in nine out of twenty-eight bone-producing samples, and cattle bones are recorded in four samples. This reverses the order of importance for these two taxa as identified by the analysis of the hand-recovered material (Table 9). This confirms that cattle, and horse, are probably over-represented in the hand-recovered assemblage, and sheep are probably significantly under-represented.

There are two associated bone groups in the sieved material, both of which appear to represent complete skeletons. A prehistoric pit (sample 59, context 553, G12) produced a neonatal cattle skeleton. All post-cranial bones are unfused, and there is no evidence for butchery, burning or scavenger gnawing.

A late Iron Age/early Roman ditch (G16, context 253, sample 16) produced a dog skeleton. All post-cranial elements are fully fused indicating that the animal is adult, but there is no evidence to suggest that it was particularly elderly. Reconstructed shoulder heights from complete limb bones, following Harcourt (1974), for this animal includes 0.45m from the right humerus (GL=138.6mm) and 0.47m from the left tibia (GL=156.3mm). Although some skeletal elements are missing it is likely that the skeleton was deposited complete, as all areas of the skeleton are represented and small bones, such as the caudal vertebrae and phalanges are also present. Cut marks are recorded around the distal shafts of the radii and tibiae, indicating that the dog was skinned before it was placed into the ditch. One lumbar vertebra exhibits osteophytes extending beyond the end of the adjacent vertebra.

Discussion

The fragmentary assemblage

The potential of the fragmentary (disarticulated) animal bone assemblage is limited by the small sample size. It can provide little information beyond a list of taxa present (Tables 8 and 11) and cannot contribute much further detail on features of the diet and economy. The assemblage is too limited to accurately assess species abundance.

The horse burial and other associated bone groups

The presence of complete and partial skeletons of animals on later prehistoric and Roman sites has been the focus of a certain amount of debate, in terms of whether they represent 'ritual' or 'rubbish' (Grant 1984; Hill 1995; Wilson 1992). These questions can be elucidated through detailed analysis of taphonomic, contextual and anatomical studies of horse skeleton deposits (eg Bendrey 2007a; Ingrem and Clark 2005; Levine et al 2002). The contextual details and disposition of the horse skeleton from Downlands suggests that this example represents 'rubbish' rather than 'ritual': the breaking of the leg bones can be associated with the process of fitting the horse into the pit, an act which might seem to be at odds with a symbolic or ritual deposit.

A palaeopathological study of the horse skeleton has indicated the possibility that the animal may have been infected with either tuberculosis or brucellosis. This is an important finding, as there is not a great deal known about bacterial diseases in animal populations; and the identification of zoonoses in animal populations is important as human populations would have contracted many diseases from their livestock. It also impacts upon the interpretation of the deposit: if the owners of the horse knew that it was diseased (which is uncertain), perhaps with a contagious infection, then it might indicate that its burial represents disease containment to prevent spread to other animals and/or humans. An alternative explanation is that the horse may have been chosen for 'ritual' burial as it was known to be diseased, and so did not represent the loss of a healthy horse to the community. However, as Knight (2001, 49–50) argues, it is not necessary to assume that a deposit need represent a sacred or profane activity, as ethnographic studies would suggest that most pre-industrial societies did not distinguish activities in such a simple dichotomy.

In addition to the horse skeleton, a neonatal cattle skeleton derived from a prehistoric pit (G12) and an adult dog skeleton from an early Roman ditch (G16). Possible interpretations of these skeletons range from ritual or symbolic depositions to the functional disposal of natural mortalities. Skinning of dogs in the Roman period is not uncommon (eg Bendrey 2002), and this does not mean that this deposit is non-ritual.

Charred plant remains
Ruth Pelling

Introduction

A series of bulk samples was taken for the recovery of environmental remains including charred plant material. Bulk samples were processed by water flotation and flots collected onto 0.5mm sieves. A series of twenty-six samples were submitted to the author for assessment of the quantity and quality of their charred plant remains. The volume of deposit processed ranged from 5 to 25 litres. The features sampled were late Bronze Age/early Iron Age or Romano-British in date and included building or levelling dumps, ditch and pit fills. A number of flots were identified as containing useful plant material, of which six were fully sorted and identified, three of late Bronze Age/early Iron Age date and three from Romano-British deposits. The assessment notes for the remaining flots are referred to in the report where appropriate.

Flots selected for detailed examination were sorted under a binocular microscope and any grain, chaff or seeds were extracted. Identification was based on morphological criteria and comparison with modern reference material and literature. Nomenclature and taxonomic order follows

Clapham *et al* (1989). Two of the Romano-British samples produced large numbers of chaff items and the small fraction flots (<1mm) were fractioned and only ¼ or ⅛ was sorted. The quantity of chaff in sample 23 was such that only half the chaff greater than 1mm was counted and identified. The figures have been altered in the table to reflect the adjusted estimated totals (adjusted figures are indicated by an asterisk).

The detailed, quantified results are displayed in Table 12. Where a fraction of the fine (<1mm) flot was sorted the totals counted are given as a separate category at the end of the table with the fraction sorted. All the samples examined produced charred material consisting of grain, chaff and weed seeds. One prehistoric sample produced waterlogged seeds.

Prehistoric deposits

Three samples of late Bronze Age/early Iron Age date were sorted and examined in full: from a deposit interpreted as a 'metalled' surface, or trackway (sample 31), the basal fill of a ditch (feature 224) forming part of a ditch complex forming the northern boundary of the prehistoric settlement (sample 9), and a pit (203) from a group of pits on the edge of the settlement (sample 1). Each sample produced a small number of cereal grains and chaff with weed seeds. Fragments of nut shell, of indeterminate species, were present in the ditch sample (sample 9). Two cereal species were identified: *Triticum spelta* (spelt wheat) and hulled *Hordeum vulgare* (barley). The chaff includes glume bases as would be expected for hulled wheats such as *Triticum spelta* , and three rachis segments of *Hordeum vulgare*. The range of cereals present would suggest *Triticum spelta* had become the wheat of choice at the site by the end of the Bronze Age with no *Triticum dicoccum* (emmer) present. *Triticum spelta* is first recorded in southern Britain in the middle Bronze Age from a few sites including Dartford, Kent (Pelling 2003), Yarnton, Oxfordshire (Mark Robinson, pers comm), and Black Patch East Sussex (Hinton 1982), although the exact timing of its introduction in different parts of the country is varied. A fairly limited weed flora includes cosmopolitan species of disturbed land (*Galium aparine, Rumex* sp, *Chenopodium album*) and grassland (*Vicia/Lathryus* sp, *Ranunculus* sp) and grasses. In addition sample 1 produced a number of possible waterlogged or recent seeds, all characteristic of disturbed sites including settlements, most notably *Urtica dioica* (stinging/common nettle).

The remaining prehistoric samples were shown on assessment to contain similar small numbers of *Triticum spelta* and *Hordeum vulgare* grain with occasional *Avena* sp (oats) which are likely to be of a wild species, with some chaff and weed seeds. No samples of this date produced dense concentrations of remains. It is likely that the majority of this charred material derives from background scatters of burnt waste which has been incorporated into the backfill of features.

The composition of the prehistoric samples with low level scatters of cereal chaff and weed seeds is typical of sites

		Late Bronze Age/Early Iron Age			Romano-British		
	Sample	1	9	31	12	21	23
	Context	203	223	363	235	285	285
	Feature	202	224			286	286
	Feature type	pit	ditch	deposit	deposit	ditch	ditch
Cereal grain							
Triticum spelta L	spelt wheat, short grain				2		3
Triticum spelta L	spelt wheat grain			13		10	14
Triticum spelta L	spelt wheat, germinated grain						7
Triticum cf *spelta* L	cf spelt wheat grain					9	13
Triticum cf *spelta* L	cf spelt wheat germinated grain					3	19
Triticum spelta/dicoccum	spelt/emmer wheat grain		2	25			5
Triticum sp	wheat, short round grain				7	26	22
Triticum sp	wheat grain		1		9	63	35
Hordeum vulgare L	barley, hulled, asymmetric grain	1					
Hordeum vulgare L	barley, hulled germinated grain					1	
Hordeum vulgare L	barley, hulled grain			1	3	7	4
Hordeum vulgare L	barley, grain	3	3	1	11	13	18
Avena sp	oats				2		2
Cerealia indet	indeterminate grain	9	5	7	41	380	476
Cereal chaff							
Triticum spelta L	spelt wheat glume base		1		155	796	1934*
Triticum spelta L	spelt wheat spikelet fork					11	26*
Triticum dicoccum L	emmer wheat glume base				1		
Triticum cf *dicoccum* L	cf emmer wheat glume base				1		6*
Triticum spelta/dicoccum	spelt/emmer wheat glume base	13	8		590	1538	3128*
Triticum spelta/dicoccum	spelt/emmer wheat spikelet fork		1	2	9	128	190*
Triticum spelta/aestivum type	spelt/bread wheat rachis internode			1	10	12	6*
Triticum sp	wheat rachis segment (internode and spikelet)	1					12*
Triticum sp	wheat rachis internode	1		2	4	4	32*
Triticum sp	wheat, basal rachis node						6*
Hordeum vulgare L	barley rachis	2	1			1	10*
cf *Hordeum vulgare*	barley, compact rachis						4*
Cerealia indet	indeterminate rachis						4*
Cereal size	culm node					1	8*
Cereal size	sprouted coleoptile				2	52	128*
Cereal size	detached embryo			1			4*
Other food plants							
Vicia/Pisum sativum L	bean/pea				1		1
cf *Linum usitatissimum*	flax seed					1	
Indet	indeterminate nut shell fragment		3				
Weeds							
Ranunculaceae							
Ranunculus acris/repens/bulbosus L	buttercup	1				3	1
Fumaria sp							1
Raphanus raphanistrum L	wild radish, capsule (broken)				1	1	1
Silene sp							1
Agrostemma githago L	corncockle						1
Stellaria media (L) Vill	chickweed				1		
Chenopodiaceae							1
Chenopodium album L	fat hen	1					
Atriplex sp	orache				1		3
Vicia/Lathyrus sp	vetch/vetchling/tare etc	1			1	6	4
Medicago/Trifolium/Lotus type	medick/clover/trefoil	2			6	8	16
Polygonaceae		1			3	5	1
Polygonum aviculare L	knotgrass					3	3
Fallopia convolvulus (L) A Love	black bindweed				2	1	1

		Late Bronze Age/Early Iron Age			Romano-British		
	Sample	1	9	31	12	21	23
	Context	203	223	363	235	285	285
	Feature	202	224			286	286
	Feature type	pit	ditch	deposit	deposit	ditch	ditch
Rumex acetosella L	sheep's sorrel	1				6	
Rumex sp	docks		1		5	21	4
Rubus sp	blackberry/raspberry etc					1	
Lithospermum arvense L	corn gromwell, silica					1	2
Odontities verna (Bell) Dumont/*Euphrasia* sp	red bartsia/eyebright				1		
Plantago media/lanceolata L	plantain				1		
Galium aparine L	goosegrass/cleavers		1				3
Compositae	small seeded in clusters (approximate)					32	
Tripleurospermum inodorum (L) Schultz Bip	scentless mayweed				1		
Leucanthemum type	corn marigold type				1		
cf *Centaurea* sp	knapweed/cornflower						1
cf *Lapsana communis* L	nipplewort					1	
Gramineae	grass, large seeded	2		1	5	24	
Gramineae	grass, small seeded	7		1	16	39	5
Poa annua L type				2			
Festuca/Lolium type	fescue/rye-grass				19	16	21
Bromus subsect *Eubromus*	brome grass			1		24	63
Bromus subsect *Eubromus*	brome grass, germinated						5
Ignota		4	3	1	7	6	17
<1mm flot, fractioned	fraction sorted					1/4	1/8
Triticum spelta L	spelt wheat glume base					7	18
Triticum spelta/dicoccum	spelt/emmer wheat glume base					349	826
Triticum spelta/dicoccum	spelt/emmer wheat spikelet fork					8	6
Triticum sp	wheat rachis internode					4	27
Hordeum vulgare L	barley rachis node						1
Cereal size	sprouted coleoptile					4	25
Cereal size	detached embryo						5
Rumex sp						2	1
Raphanus raphanistrum L	wild radish, capsule (broken)					1	
Cruciferae						1	
Chenopodiaceae/Caryophyllaceae	plantain					5	
Chenopodium album L	fat hen						1
Atriplex sp	orache					1	
Polygonum aviculare L	knotgrass						1
Rumex acetosella L	sheep's sorrel					1	
Plantago media/lanceolata L	plantain					1	1
Labiatae, small seeded						1	1
Rubbiaceae indet						1	
Medicago/Trifolium/Lotus type	medick/clover/trefoil					9	7
Leucanthemum sp type	corn marigold type					1	1
Tripleurospermum inodorum (L) Schultz Bip	scentless mayweed					1	4
Poa annua type						11	
Festuca/Lolium type	fescue/rye-grass					1	
Gramineae	small seeded grass					5	10
Ignota						7	2
Waterlogged seeds							
Urtica dioica L	stinging/common nettle	+++					
Aphanes arvensis L	parsley piert	+					
Stellaria media (L) Vill	chickweed	+					
Rubus sp (frags)	blackberry/raspberry etc	+					
Gramineae	small seeded grass	+					

Table 12. Charred and waterlogged plant remains. * = adjusted figure; +++ = abundant; + = present.

73

involved in routine day to day processing and consumption of cereals. Given the potential for contamination by late Roman material and the fact that day to day preparation and consumption of grain occurs on all sites (eg van der Veen and Jones 2006) it is not possible to assess the scale of processing or consumption involved.

Later Romano-British deposits

Three samples of Romano-British period deposit were sorted and examined in full, two from the fill of boundary ditch 286 (samples 21 and 23) associated with the aisled building and one from a dump of levelling material formed to create a platform for the aisled building (sample 12). All three samples produced large numbers of cereal remains, particularly the ditch samples in which chaff, particularly glume bases, was abundant. Grain tended to be poorly preserved reflected in the high number of indeterminate grains. The preservation of chaff was extremely variable, in part presumably a reflection of the vast numbers preserved. Weed seeds were present but in small numbers compared to grain and particularly the chaff.

As in the previous phase the cereals identified were *Triticum spelta* and hulled *Hordeum vulgare*, the principal cereals of the Romano-British period. Occasional glume bases of *Triticum dicoccum* suggest a second wheat may have been cultivated or was merely present as a weed of the *T spelta* crop. The *Triticum spelta* grains tended to be rather short, although clear indications of being held in tight glumes confirm they are derived from a hulled wheat. A number of short round *Triticum* grains which did not display the characteristic ridges and constriction marks of hulled wheat were recorded as *Triticum* sp and may theoretically include free-threshing wheat. The presence of short grained *Triticum spelta* would, however, suggest they are of the same species. The occurrence of short grained *Triticum spelta* and *Triticum dicoccum* has been noted at a number of other Romano-British sites including Tiddington, Warwickshire (Moffett 1986) and Mansfield College, Oxford (Pelling 2000a). It is likely that ancient populations of hulled wheat showed a much greater genetic variation either within individual populations or from one population to another. A number of grains of *Triticum spelta* and one *Hordeum vulgare* had germinated. It is likely that the large number of poorly preserved indeterminate grain had also germinated. In addition five grains of *Bromus* subsect *Eubromus*, a large seeded grass which commonly occurs as a contaminant of cereal grain, had also germinated. Other crops were rare but included a possible seed of *Linum usitatissimum* (flax) and two pulses of indeterminate species.

Chaff was abundant in all three Romano-British samples but exceedingly so in the two boundary ditch deposits associated with the aisled building. A third sample from the same feature (sample 21, feature 286) was noted on assessment to contain a similar composition of grain, frequent glume bases and few weed seeds. All three samples are likely to have derived from the same dump of material. Glume bases

of *Triticum spelta* or poorly preserved *Triticum spelta/ dicoccum* dominated, with in excess of 12,000 glume bases (adjusted figure) in sample 23. In addition rachis internodes, basal rachis fragments and complete rachis segments were counted suggesting that whole ears of *Triticum spelta* were represented from which the grain had been largely removed. Occasional rachis of *Hordeum vulgare* (barley), culm nodes (straw nodes) and several sprouted embryos ('coleoptiles') were also present. The number of weeds in the ditch samples was very low in relation to grain or chaff, suggesting semi-clean ears or spikelets are represented. The large proportion of chaff in relation to grain and weed seeds would indicate some sort of processing waste is represented here. The presence of germinated grain and sprouted 'coleoptiles' raises the possibility that the waste derives from malting of the spelt wheat. The fact that only a relatively small proportion of grain shows signs of having sprouted is to be expected in the waste by-product as this would include the failed grain.

The malting of wheat for beer was known to the Romans (Pliny, Book XVIII). Grain would be steeped in water until it was swollen, then turned out on to the floor where it was allowed to germinate. Once the sprouts ('coleoptiles') had reached the length of the grain the process was stopped by roasting the grain in hot air (up to 104°C, above which the diastase enzymes, which help convert starch into sugar for the growing plant, become denatured). Several examples of possible malting waste have been identified from Roman period sites, particularly from corn-driers (van der Veen 1989; Pearson and Robinson 1994) where the chaff and sprouts from malted spelt grain (the 'comings') removed after the malted grain had been parched appear to be used for fuel in subsequent episodes. The published examples also tend to produce small proportions of weeds suggesting the spikelets have been cleaned before hand. A similar deposit was recovered from a pit in Alcester, Warwickshire (Pelling 2000b) in which 25 per cent of the grain could positively be identified as having germinated and a number of coleoptiles were recovered. Large deposits of similar material were carefully sampled and examined from corn-driers associated with an aisled building at Grateley, Hampshire (Campbell 2008) in which large numbers of coleoptiles and germinated grain were recovered including *in situ* examples of grain probably being heated to halt the malting process. It is likely that malting was fairly widespread but that it is only recognized if conducted on a large scale, as occurs with some corn-driers. In the current example the comings may simply have been burnt for disposal purposes or used as fuel before being discarded in the ditch. The association of the features in which the deposits were found and the aisled building would suggest that grain storage or processing was taking place in the building, as appears to have been the case at Grateley (Campbell 2008).

The limited weed flora was dominated by species of open ground and disturbed habitats such as *Raphanus raphanistrum* (wild radish), *Plantago lanceolata/media* (plantain), *Stellaria media agg* (chickweed), *Atriplex* sp (orache), *Polygonum aviculare* (knotgrass), *Odontites verna* (eyebright) and *Tripleurospermum inodorum* (scentless mayweed). One characteristic cornfield weed recorded in this phase, *Agrostemma githago* (corn cockle) is regarded as a Roman introduction. There is no indication in the weed flora for the cultivation of heavy clay or chalk soils. In contrast a few species are more indicative of lighter soils including *Rumex acetosella* (sorrel), *Tripleurospermum inodorum* and *Fumaria* sp (fumitory). A number of grasses are also present, particularly large seeded varieties such as *Bromus* subsect *Eubromus* and smaller seeded *Festuca/Lolium* type.

The low number of weed seeds other than cereal-sized grasses in the Romano-British period deposits is striking and would suggest that the bulk of weeds had been removed prior to the malting process. It has been suggested on the basis of the composition of samples at Iron Age sites in the Thames valley and Hampshire chalk, that the removal of weeds prior to storage of spikelets (and consequently final processing stages such as malting) is associated with storage patterns and available labour force (Stevens 2003). Where a large seasonal labour force was available spikelets could be cleaned of the bulk of their weeds prior to storage. This might be expected on a site large enough to support a substantial corn-drier for example and would explain why weed seeds are limited in

the deposits at Grateley. On a smaller subsistence farmstead where labour was limited, the removal of weed seeds might take place at the final stages of cleaning during day to day processing of the grain and the majority of deposits would consist of more equal mixes of chaff and weed seeds with occasional grain.

Conclusions

The analysis of archaeobotanical samples from Downlands indicates that the cereals cultivated remained constant from the late Bronze Age into the Romano-British period, with spelt wheat and barley being dominant. It is likely that a change of scale of cereal production occurred by the Romano-British period possibly related to an increased labour force and presumably reflected in the presence of an aisled building. The Romano-British samples from the ditch complex associated with the aisled building contain the waste product of one or more episodes of crop processing which may include the malting of the spelt wheat, the waste product or 'comings' consisting of the chaff and sprouted embryos (coleoptiles).

5
Discussion

Much work has been done on the archaeology of the late Bronze Age and the early to middle Iron Age in Britain, particularly in the central southern region of England, where the hillforts and settlements of the chalk downlands of Dorset, Hampshire, Sussex and Wiltshire have been extensively studied. Elsewhere significant work has been carried out on a number of sites identifying regional variations. However in Kent the picture has been less good and in 1979, at a national conference on the archaeology of Kent, it was noted that there had been few excavations of sites of this period and that very few of these had been published (Champion 1982, 31; Cunliffe 1982, 40).

In a more recent review Tim Champion is more optimistic (2007a, 293–6), indicating the increasing quantity of data being produced as a result of the implementation of Planning Policy Guidance Note 16 (PPG16 1990) and the appointment of a County Archaeologist for Kent in 1989. However, he notes that much of this data resides in grey literature client reports, that it is often fragmentary in nature and that still few sites have been published. Planning-led excavation is inevitably focused where development is occurring and this biases the data to certain regions of the county: the chalk downlands and the High Weald have been far less intensively studied than the Thames corridor, north Kent coast, Thanet and, to a lesser degree, the Greensand vale between Folkestone and Maidstone. The data is further limited by its concentration on development which rarely allows complete excavation of archaeological sites. Champion goes on to note that problems of chronology and terminology remain and that a picture of the development of Kent in the later prehistoric period will only emerge with the increasing excavation and publication of sites to modern standards.

Against this background, the discovery of settlement dating to the latest phase of the Bronze Age or earliest Iron Age extending up to the beginning of the middle Iron Age at Downlands is of regional importance. Although the area of excavation only located the periphery of the site and little can be deduced about its size, nature and development, it has produced a reasonably sized assemblage of pottery which will contribute to the growing corpus of material from this period. Unfortunately the site yielded only one prehistoric object of metal and no radiocarbon datable material to assist with the pottery analysis, but the material is still of value in its associations of forms and fabrics. Further its presence

will add to the understanding of settlement patterns within the county, which is at an embryonic stage. Environmental data from the site was also limited with only three prehistoric samples producing charred plant remains worthy of detailed study. Even these three samples are not entirely secure in their provenance and the evidence derived from them must be viewed with some caution.

Our knowledge of the Roman period in Kent is much greater than for the prehistoric period, in part due to the availability of written sources, but also due to the identification and excavation of many more sites across the county. However much of what Champion says about the prehistoric period is applicable to the Roman period, particularly in relation to the rural economy and settlement pattern, which Millett (2007, 138) notes is still poorly understood. Study of the archaeology of the period has largely focused on the prestigious sites, the urban centres, forts and villas, the latter concentrated to the west of the county, and on the extensive burial evidence, but has largely overlooked the native farmsteads and settlements, which must have occupied much of the landscape. What work has been done has again tended to focus on the areas of greatest development along the Thames corridor, the north Kent coast and around existing urban centres, though to a lesser degree than for the study of prehistoric settlement.

The presence of an aisled building, and by inference a villa or comparatively wealthy farm, at Downlands is a valuable addition to our knowledge of the settlement pattern of the east of the county, where few masonry buildings are known. It is unfortunate that the excavated area lies on the periphery of the site and as a result gives only a tantalising hint of the extent and status of the settlement. It is therefore only possible to make generalised statements about the site's development and importance in this period.

The prehistoric period

The late Bronze Age and early to middle Iron Age in Kent

The middle and late Bronze Age in Britain saw an intensification of land use from the middle of the second millennium continuing into the early part of the first millennium BC. Large scale ritual sites and monumental burials disappear from the archaeological record and fixed settlements and field boundaries appear in the landscape (Yates 2001, 65). This development is thought to have been accompanied by a shift in power and wealth from the upland areas to the lowland zone in eastern England, particularly around the Thames, shown mostly clearly in the distribution of metal hoards (Champion 1982, 34–8).

During the middle Bronze Age settlement typically consisted of small groups of round-houses with associated features including pits, ponds and four-post structures – generally interpreted as granaries (Brück 1999, 145). These settlements are thought to represent single family units and none are large enough to be considered to be nucleated or village settlements. This pattern appears to continue into the late Bronze Age, but with an increase in diversity of site types emerging and with indications that the scale of some sites may increase (Brück 2007, 26). Early Iron Age settlement sites are more elusive than those of the Bronze Age, though this may be as much to do with shortcomings in our understanding, and sites of this date are increasingly being identified (Haselgrove and Pope 2007, 5). What evidence exists suggests similar types of settlement, but with increased emphasis on 'communal' sites (ibid, 18) and a greater longevity of use, indicated by replacement of round-houses (Brück 2007, 29).

Both enclosed and unenclosed settlements are found in the late Bronze Age and early Iron Age. Enclosures vary in form some are ditched, sometimes accompanied by a bank, others palisaded or walled (Cunliffe 1991, 28ff). A few more substantial enclosures located on hilltops may represent the beginnings of hillforts and the societal changes which led to their construction in the Iron Age. In the east of England a specialised defensive enclosure type, often called 'ringworks' has been identified (ibid, 39–40). These are typified by substantial circular earthworks, between c 30 and 150m in diameter, within which round-houses, pits and fenced off areas can be identified. This type of enclosure has been identified in Essex at Springfield Lyons (Buckley and Hedges 1987), Mucking South (Jones and Bond 1980) and North (Bond 1988) and Hornchurch (Guttmann and Last 2000), but is clearly distributed across much of the south-east and into the East Midlands. The only example of a 'ringwork' from Kent was excavated at Mill Hill, Deal (Stebbing 1934; Champion 1980, 233–7), about 1.5km north-west of the site of the current excavation at Downlands. These circular enclosures have been suggested to be a specialised class of a more general enclosure type such as the rectangular enclosure at Lofts Farm, Essex (Brown 1988) and Highstead, enclosure B70. Other less regular enclosures in the area may also fall into this category (Champion 2007b, 285).

In Kent field systems form the bulk of the evidence of settlement for the late Bronze Age. They have been identified along the lower reaches of the Thames and the east coast as far as the Isle of Thanet, reflecting a pattern observed to the north of the Thames in Essex and further up river to the west (Yates 2001). Many of these sites appear to concentrate on the river valleys feeding into the Thames and its estuary or onto the north Kent coast. Sites of this period are also beginning to be found along the Greensand vale beneath the scarp slope of the North Downs between Folkestone and Maidstone (Champion 2007a, 298). These field systems are argued to represent a rise in pastoralism and a growing density of population (Pryor 1998, 82; Yates 2001).

The settlements associated with these field systems have proved more elusive in Kent and no sites have been discovered to compare with the extensive field system and settlement site excavated at Hornchurch in Essex (Guttmann and Last 2000). The scant evidence available suggests that some of the Kent sites had open settlement associated, but this by its nature can be difficult to identify. Unenclosed occupation has been suggested at Monkton Court Farm, Thanet (Perkins et al 1994) and South Street and Radfall Corner on the A299 Thanet Way amongst others, mainly in the east of the county. Enclosed settlements have also been identified, again concentrated to the east of Kent, such as the group of enclosures excavated at Highstead, Chislet near Canterbury (Bennett et al 2007) and South Dumpton Down, Broadstairs on Thanet (Perkins 1995).

The distribution of sites in the late Bronze Age shows a strong bias to the Thames corridor, north Kent coast and the Isle of Thanet. Few sites have been identified on the North Downs, but as noted this reflects the absence of archaeological fieldwork on the chalk downs. The bulk of the evidence from the downs comes from road or pipeline schemes and so provides only a tantalising glimpse of the record. Occupation contemporary with Mill Hill, Deal has been identified at site 5 on the A2 Bridge to Barham by-pass (Macpherson-Grant 1980) and late Bronze Age field boundaries observed at Venson Road on the Whitfield–Eastry improvement road (Rady 1995), 5km east of Downlands. Numerous aerial photographs indicate further activity throughout the downs and the distribution of sites on the chalk downlands of Sussex suggests that more settlements await discovery in this region (Cunliffe 1991, 28).

The end of the Bronze Age and earliest Iron Age has been identified as a dynamic period of intense change with new socio-economic systems developing across Britain (Cunliffe 1991, 61). This is most clearly represented in the pottery tradition with the emergence of distinct regional groupings by the sixth to fifth centuries BC. These changes are further evidenced by the development of hillforts across central southern England and into Wales. The period leading up to this is thought to mark a decline in population, possibly linked to over exploitation of land in the late Bronze Age and deterioration in the weather (Cunliffe 1991, 57–9), the population only beginning to recover from around 800 BC onwards.

In Kent these changes are reflected by the appearance of a distinctive pottery group identified at Highstead and dated to around 500–350 BC (Couldrey 2007, 169–70). This group has been identified at up to thirty other sites in east Kent and termed the 'east Kent rusticated tradition' (Macpherson-Grant 1991), though it is suggested that the presence of rustication may not be the defining characteristic of this assemblage (Bryan 2002; Champion 2007a, 297). The pottery group shows clear influence from continental pottery observed in north France, particularly on the Channel Tunnel sites (Blancquaert and Bostyn 1998).

The changes in society are also reflected in changes in settlement and land use. Early Iron Age sites have yet to be identified in the west of the county and are not common in the east with few late Bronze Age settlements showing continuity into the early Iron Age (Yates 2001; Champion 2007a, 302), Highstead being the main exception to date (Champion 2007b). The field systems appear to have fallen out of use at about the same time as these settlements, a situation observed to the north of the Thames, in Essex, and along the lower and middle reaches of the Thames, and there is little evidence to indicate subsequent occupation of the areas in which they were located (Wymer and Brown 1995, 157; Yates 1991; Champion 2007a, 299–300). One exception to this may be Underdown Lane, Herne Bay (Jarman 2005), where suspected early to middle Iron Age round-houses have been identified a short distance from a large late Bronze Age enclosure and associated ditches (Shand 2002; Jarman and Shand 2003), though there is no evidence to suggest that the land divisions themselves remained in use.

The nature and distribution of the settlements of the early Iron Age in Kent is unclear, though it is likely that they were similar in appearance to those of the late Bronze Age. The majority of the identified sites have been located as a result of evaluation trenching or 'corridor' type schemes, such as the A2 Bridge to Barham by-pass (Macpherson Grant 1980) and the Whitfield–Eastry improvement road (Parfitt et al 1997), or pipelines such as the Stourmouth to Adisham water main (Ogilvie 1960), the Herne Bay waste water pipeline (Parfitt 1995b) or the Sandwich Bay waste water scheme (Hearne et al 1995). Although these have indicated extensive occupation of the landscape they provide only limited evidence of the nature of settlement. Large scale excavation has only occurred at a few sites, notably Highstead (Bennett et al 2007) and South Dumpton Down near Broadstairs, Thanet (Perkins 1995).

At Highstead round-houses post-dating the late Bronze Age have been identified in an open settlement. The only comparable site, yielding a cluster of round-houses, may be the nearby site at Underdown Lane (Jarman 2005). Otherwise identification of structures is rare. Open settlements have been identified at site 1 on the A2 Bridge to Barham by-pass (Macpherson-Grant 1980), Dolland's Moor and Castle Hill, Folkestone (Rady et al forthcoming), all to the east of Canterbury, and White Horse Stone on the Channel Tunnel Rail Link (Oxford Archaeological Unit 2000a; 2001a) located on the east bank of the River Medway, the most westerly site of this period found to date. None has produced good evidence for structures. Enclosed settlements have been identified at Church Whitfield, near Dover (Parfitt et al 1997), site 8 on the A2 Bridge to Barham by-pass (Macpherson-Grant 1980) and on Thanet at Dumpton Gap (Hurd 1909), South Dumpton Down (Perkins 1995) and

North Foreland (Diack 2003), all close to Broadstairs, and Hartsdown (Perkins 1996) and Fort Hill (Perkins 1997, 227), both at Margate.

Many of the early Iron Age sites of east Kent do not appear to last far into the middle Iron Age. By the fourth century BC Highstead shows no sign of occupation (Bennett et al 2007) and this is reflected at a number of other sites. At North Foreland there is some evidence of later middle Iron Age to late Iron Age occupation, but only at Bigbury, near Canterbury has good evidence of middle Iron Age occupation been recovered and here there is no evidence of earlier occupation (Thompson 1983). However there are problems in identifying ceramic assemblages of this date in the east of the county and so the chronology of this period is unclear (Champion 2007a, 297). Conversely to the west of the county the middle Iron Age ceramic tradition has been better established and sites of this period are therefore known, though still not frequent. Best known are the hillforts of the High Weald, but other sites have been identified at Farningham Hill (Philp 1984) and Greenhithe (Detsicas 1966) both of which produced evidence for enclosures.

The apparent shift in settlement pattern or density at the beginning of the Iron Age and in the middle Iron Age, indicated by these changes, is not well understood. It is unclear to what extent it is associated with population decline, shifting focus of settlement or changes in the nature of settlement and land use leading to its becoming less visible in the archaeological landscape, or indeed whether it is simply the selectivity of our current data.

The chronology of Downlands

The prehistoric occupation at Downlands has been principally dated on the basis of the ceramic assemblage retrieved from intensive pitting. The pottery indicates the main phase of occupation to lie between about 600 and 350 BC. This dating is based largely on the ceramic sequence established by Couldrey at Highstead (Couldrey 2007) and other sites, and identified by Macpherson-Grant at up to thirty sites in east Kent (Macpherson-Grant 1990; 1991; 1997) and in more recent studies at Dumpton Gap (Bryan 2002), Saltwood Tunnel and Beechbrook Wood (Edgeley-Long 2006a; 2006b), and White Horse Stone (Morris 2006).

The larger part of the pottery assemblage from Downlands shows traits consistent with the 'east Kent rusticated tradition', dated to 500–350 BC. However the small but significant quantity of late Bronze Age decorated phase pottery present suggests that the site had an earlier origin in the very late Bronze Age or earliest Iron Age, around the eighth to seventh century BC, with a probable emphasis on the latter part of the period. It is suggested that the site therefore shows continuity from the latest Bronze Age or earliest Iron Age into the early to middle Iron Age.

The chronology provided by the east Kent ceramic style is in need of refinement and its end point in particular is not clearly dated (Champion 2007a, 296–7). Pottery associations with sites outside the county, particularly at

Danebury (Brown 2000), suggest that some vessels within the assemblage might date to later than 350 BC, though how much later is not clear. This late date for the end of the sequence at the site is supported by the finding of a La Tène I pin brooch, dated by parallels to the fourth to third century BC, in close association with several of the larger assemblages of pottery from the site. Although these are considered to be derived from redeposited rubbish dumps from elsewhere on the site it seems reasonable to suggest a broadly contemporary date for the pottery and the brooch.

The precise chronological relationship to the distribution of late Bronze Age or earliest Iron Age sites in the region remains uncertain as none have precise chronological sequences for establishment, development and disuse. The date range provided by the pottery suggests that the site at Downlands was broadly contemporary with Highstead (phases 2, 3a and 3b) (Bennett *et al* 2007). It also suggests a possible overlap in occupation between Downlands and the 'ringwork' at Mill Hill, Deal, and possibly with the latest phase of occupation at Chalk Hill, Ramsgate (Shand 2001a; 2001b; McNee 2006), along with several other sites in the area. The chronology of the site appears to follow that set out for the late Bronze Age and early Iron Age by Champion (2007a), outlined above, and the absence of middle to late Iron Age pottery accords with the data from other sites in the region. It is tempting therefore to suggest that the establishment of settlement at Downlands is associated with the move away from the field systems and the apparent shift in settlement pattern observed at the end of the Bronze Age.

The setting of Downlands within the prehistoric landscape

The positioning of the site on high ground overlooking the coastal area on the approach to the Wantsum channel reflects the clustering of sites identified around the Reculver peninsula and on the land on either side of the channel in the late Bronze Age (Yates 2001). The density of settlement apparent in these regions has not yet been identified to the east of the Stour or on the southern side of the east mouth of the Wantsum channel, but this is as likely due to selectivity of data as it is to a real absence of settlement in the late Bronze Age. The position of Downlands about 1.5km from the only definite 'ringwork' in Kent at Mill Hill, Deal, suggests that another concentration of sites is to be expected. The general topography of the area suggests some similarity with that around Highstead; elevated ground looking across marsh to open water, with a hinterland of rolling hills cut by river valleys. However as yet no field systems comparable to those of the north Kent coast and Thames corridor have been identified in the vicinity.

Aerial photography and the work of antiquarians indicates the potential for a complex landscape around Downlands, but only one of these sites has been investigated. Aerial photographs have identified a large oval enclosure *c* 300m south-west of the site, assigned to the late Bronze

Age (SMR TR 34 NE 58), 300m further south lie a trackway and ring-ditch (SMR TR 34 NE 70), the latter presumed to be a Bronze Age barrow, and *c* 0.5km to the south-east, on Hawkshill Down, another large oval enclosure, for which no date has been advanced (SMR TR 34 NE 47). In 1880 Petrie recorded the presence of banks at Hawkshill Close to the south of Walmer Castle, *c* 800m east of Downlands (Petrie 1880, 13). These he suggested formed part of an ancient field system. A rectangular enclosure was recorded by Hasted, 600m south-west of Downlands (Hasted 1798, 565) and in 1982 a series of soil marks was investigated in this area revealing a possible enclosure, but no dating evidence was recovered (Keith Parfitt, pers comm). Without investigation of these features the data cannot be confidently interpreted, but it does lend support to the suggested presence of a focus of activity in this region.

No study of the early Iron Age settlement pattern of Kent comparable with Yates' study of the Thames valley and estuary in the Bronze Age (Yates 2001) has been published. Occupation of this period being until recently noted as much for its absence from the record as for any pattern of settlement. It is therefore difficult to discuss the site in relation to contemporary settlement and land use in this period. Few sites on the north Kent coast show signs of occupation in the early Iron Age, the main identified sites being Highstead and Underdown Lane. Highstead again bears comparison with Downlands; here open settlement in the Iron Age followed the enclosures of the late Bronze Age, notably defended enclosure B70, likened to the 'ringwork' enclosures (Champion 2007b, 285) and we should maybe look for a parallel with the Mill Hill 'ringwork' falling out of use and being replaced by unenclosed or less substantially enclosed settlement. The focus at Mill Hill perhaps moved away to the higher ground around Downlands.

It is possible that Downlands belongs with a group of early Iron Age sites identified in recent work occupying coastal, or near coastal locations, though this pattern is not widely dissimilar to the late Bronze Age distribution around the Wantsum channel and so may not be of great significance. The principal site of this date on the mainland is again that at Highstead. On Thanet early Iron Age settlement enclosures are distributed around the coastal fringe at Dumpton Gap (Hurd 1909) and South Dumpton Down, (Perkins 1995), North Foreland (Diack 2003), all at Broadstairs, Hartsdown (Perkins 1996) and Fort Hill (Perkins 1997, 227), both at Margate, and settlement is indicated at Ebbsfleet (Hearne *et al* 1995), on the south coast opposite Downlands. To the south of Downlands, at Folkestone, work on the Channel Tunnel terminal has located settlement at Castle Hill and Dolland's Moor with a more general spread of activity across the area (Rady *et al* forthcoming). The proximity of these sites to the coast suggests the exploitation of the sea, the coastal plain and its hinterland. Access to the sea would have provided a strong communication link with other coastal settlements both in Britain and abroad and the similarities of the local pottery with continental traditions has already been noted. How these coastal sites related to each other and to inland settlement is not apparent, but the similarity of the ceramic tradition has been argued to imply a cultural zone (Macpherson-Grant 1990, 63) and this could be centred along the coastal fringe of east Kent.

The positioning of the Castle Hill and Dolland's Moor sites on the edge of the North Downs at an elevation of around 40–50m OD overlooking the coastal plain at Folkestone, has been noted (Rady et al forthcoming) and is reminiscent of the position of Downlands. As at Downlands both these sites yielded background quantities of late Bronze Age pottery suggesting earlier activity, but no features were identified. Whether this represents a move to high ground on the edge of the downs, or to a greater exploitation of the entire area of the downs, during the very late Bronze Age or earliest Iron Age, cannot be deduced from the available data, but might help explain the current gap in our knowledge of settlement patterns.

The nature and extent of settlement

As with most of the sites producing evidence of occupation in the late Bronze Age and early to middle Iron Age in Kent only a small proportion of the site has been observed and so it is not possible to discuss the form and development of the site itself in any detail.

The extent of the site is unclear but watching brief work in the vicinity has produced evidence for contemporary occupation. Early to middle Iron Age occupation was discovered less than 100m to the west of the site, at No 429 Dover Road, during a watching brief conducted by Canterbury Archaeological Trust (Parfitt 1997b). Four pits were recorded, yielding pottery, burnt flint and two burials. The burials, of a child and a juvenile, were deposited within what were described as disused storage pits. Further to the south, c 500m from the site, a four-post structure and ditch of Iron Age date were recorded during a watching brief on a pipeline adjacent to the A258 (Dover Road) by Dover Archaeological Group (Parfitt 1981). Whether these formed part of the same settlement is not determinable, but seems probable, suggesting a wide area of occupation extending west of the site and up the slope to its south towards the crest of the hill. Whether this indicates a shifting pattern of settlement within the landscape or a dispersed but contemporary one is a matter of speculation.

That the site at Downlands represents settlement is strongly indicated by the presence of domestic pottery types and by the small assemblage of mammal bone recovered from the pits. Whether the settlement was open or enclosed cannot be determined with certainty, but the presence of the boundary ditch sequence to the north suggests the latter. The pottery recovered from the ditches indicates that they may not have lasted throughout the life of the site and it is possible that the early Iron Age saw an unenclosed phase, as at Highstead and elsewhere. However it is also possible that the boundary remained in some form, fenced or hedged, as there is little trace of activity to its north in the later period despite an apparent rise in intensity of activity suggested

by the ceramic record. That the boundary ditches were associated with a field system cannot be precluded, but there is no evidence as yet to suggest such an association.

The intensive nature of pitting at the site is not reflected at other sites in the area and is not a feature of the period elsewhere, where the pattern is usually more scattered with only limited intercutting of features. The activity or activities represented by this pitting are unclear, but its intensity seems to have become greater towards the latter end of the early Iron Age. This may suggest expansion of population, putting pressure on the space within the enclosure, but other reasons may be advanced and without a clear understanding of the function of the pits it is unwise to draw conclusions. The intensity and longevity of the pitting suggests the possibility of zoning of activity within the enclosure, although it is possible that the activity itself changed over time. Initially the pitting may have been aimed at quarrying brickearth and gravel from the solifluxion deposits present in the area, but later on a different function must be sought.

The economy of Downlands

The evidence for the economy of the site is limited, but it is assumed that the site was principally agricultural in nature. The presence of bones from horse, cattle and sheep in small quantities does not allow any significant conclusions to be drawn and the state of preservation was poor, suggesting that much of this material had decayed. However some degree of pastoralism may be inferred, possibly supported by the presence of a clay weight probably used in weaving. As noted above the environmental samples from the site are not securely stratified and so the presence of cereal grain, chaff, pulses and crop weeds in several of the infills of pits must be viewed with caution. The limited quantity of evidence available suggests that cereal processing may have been taking place, with the main crops being spelt wheat and hulled barley. However the quantity and composition of the material is typical of domestic sites on which grain was being prepared and consumed and little can be inferred about the nature and extent of growing and processing. The limited weed seed evidence available produced evidence for grassland and weeds of disturbed ground – the latter being in keeping with the extensive pitting observed across much of the site. Champion notes that it has been suggested that the move away from the field enclosures of the late Bronze Age might signify a shift from pastoralism to arable farming (Champion 2007a, 300) and it is possible that the evidence reflects an increased reliance on crops. The presence of a rubbing or quern stone within one of the pits certainly infers crop processing was taking place.

The position of the site overlooking the Lydden valley and close to the coast suggests that the site would have utilised the resources available from these environments but there is no evidence for their exploitation in the archaeological record.

It has been tentatively suggested that pottery was being produced at Downlands, though this has left no direct trace.

The range of pottery fabrics at Downlands, though wide, was not as great as at other sites of the period. This may indicate a reliance on a more limited source of pottery, possibly locally produced, and a superficial analysis of the fabrics suggests the clay source of many sherds to be similar. The raw materials for manufacture are largely available locally and it has been tentatively suggested that production was occurring at the site, though this has left no physical trace.

There is also a small quantity of metalworking residue from the site, including hammerscale, smithing slag and bloomery slag, recovered from Iron Age deposits and thought to be fairly securely dated. This suggests that metalworking was taking place at the site, but in the absence of other supporting evidence little can be deduced about its nature and importance to the local economy. The evidence suggests that both bronzeworking and ironworking may have taken place.

The Roman period

Kent in the Roman period

The settlement pattern in Kent at the beginning of the Roman period is generally accepted to owe much to the late Iron Age pattern of settlement (Detsicas 1983, 9, 38, 83–4; Todd 1982, 51; Millett 2007, 139–41). That the principal towns at Canterbury (*Durovernum Cantiacorum*) and Rochester (*Durobrivae*) were built on or close to tribal centres is well attested and that the minor town at Springhead (*Vagniacae*) also had its origins in the late Iron Age seems clear. Similarly many villas and other lesser sites had late Iron Age precursors. The origin of the harbours and forts at Reculver (*Regulbium*), Richborough (*Rutupiae*), Dover (*Dubris*) and Port Lympne (*Lemanis*) are less clear. Other small towns or settlements, such as those at Crayford (*Noviomagus*) and Dartford on the line of Watling Street, as yet show no sign of late Iron Age occupation and may owe their origin to the introduction of the Roman road system.

Millett (2007, 139) notes that the late Iron Age appears to have seen an increasing importance of coastal sites and in particular notes the importance of estuarine sites, several of which later grew into Roman centres (*ibid*, 146–7). He goes on to suggest that the settlement pattern of the north and north-east coasts in the late Iron Age was dominated by the river systems and their access to the sea and also notes the importance of the coast along either side of the Wantsum channel. The excavation of a cemetery site at Mill Hill, Deal (Parfitt 1995a), with its warrior burials and the discovery of a 'crown', clearly suggests an important settlement focus in the area around the Lydden valley, not far from Downlands, suggesting this pattern to extend at least this far around the east coast.

The late Iron Age pattern of settlement along the Thames corridor and north Kent coast appears to be reflected in the distribution of villas in the west of the county. Here villas and other buildings are focused largely in the river valleys of the Cray, Darent and Medway, where a number of villas and other buildings have been investigated, and to a lesser degree on the dip slope of the North Downs close to the estuary and coast. East of the Medway the distribution is very different; a few villas and other buildings are known along the north coast as far as Faversham, where a small concentration has been noted, but few have been recorded further east and the Stour valley remains remarkably free of buildings. To the south of the North Downs few sites have been located outside the major river valleys of the west. The only sizable villa discovered to date is at Folkestone, and apart from a few buildings on its fringes none are known from the Weald. Of the buildings discovered in the east of the county none are on the scale of Darenth or Eccles, most appearing to be quite modest – though few have been thoroughly excavated and recorded to modern standards.

Though now somewhat out of date, the late Dr Alec Detsicas provided a good account of the known masonry buildings of Kent, divided into farms and villa-estates, generally on the basis of size, and isolated bath-houses and temples (Detsicas 1983, 83–153). However the status of many of these sites remains unresolved as few have been subject to thorough investigation and very few to modern excavation. Not all accounts accept the status of all of these building as villas, or the division of farm and villa-estate, and so there are disparities in the exact distribution between authors, though the general trends remain the same.

The reasons for the apparent variation in distribution of villas have been the subject of much debate, but no clear conclusions have been drawn (Todd 1982; Black 1987; Andrews 2001; Millett 2007 for summaries). The development of villas and their role in the economy of the countryside has also been the subject of extensive discussion. Millett warns against assumptions about the role of villas, pointing out that land ownership was the key to power in the Roman world, allowing access to political office, rather than necessarily being the source of wealth. Further there are dangers in drawing conclusions from individual sites, where factors of individual fortune play an important role. The construction of a villa in the Roman style was, Millett suggests, a statement of aspiration, but its presence does not necessarily suggest a particular economic model and the underlying pattern of settlement which formed the basis of the rural economy is still not well understood.

A recent study of Thanet by Perkins (2001) has contributed significantly to our knowledge of the settlement of the island. Detsicas' account only identified one possible villa or farm on Thanet at Margate. Perkins however has identified twenty-three sites across the island possessing signs of masonry structures, most notably the substantial villa at Minster-in-Thanet, which is the subject of seasonal excavation by the Kent Archaeological Society. Not all of these sites are unequivocally villas; three are suggested to be temples and others are only represented by scatters of building material or cropmarks, but they do indicate a greater concentration of higher status building than had previously been accepted. A further twenty-six sites show evidence for occupation, the status of which is not always certain, but many appear to be farmsteads or small settlements. This study is important in demonstrating the density of settlement and in indicating the limitations of our knowledge. There is little reason to suggest that the density of settlement on Thanet is not reflected on the mainland.

The villa, even in its most basic form, did not represent the norm of settlement. Most of the population must have lived in small farmsteads or settlements with timber buildings, such as the recently excavated sites at Westhawk Farm, Ashford (Booth 2001) and Eddington Farm, Herne Bay (Jarman and Shand 2003), and the economic and social relationship of the general population with those in the villas is not easily deduced from the available evidence. Only a few such sites have been studied thoroughly and published, although the evidence for their presence is scattered across much of the county. The biased picture of settlement given by the distribution of villas is further suggested by the distribution of burials, many of which must imply high status individuals. It would seem appropriate to call for a much more thorough study of the underlying settlement and economic pattern represented by these lesser settlements on the mainland of Kent, along the lines of Perkins' study of Thanet.

The setting of Downlands within the Roman landscape

Downlands lies midway between the major Roman ports of Richborough and Dover, c 6km east of the main road linking them (Margary 1955, route 100, 33–4). The site occupies a commanding position looking across the mouth of the Wantsum channel to the Isle of Thanet. To its south and west the rolling hills of the downs would have provided good agricultural land and a plentiful supply of wood for fuel and building. To the north the site overlooks the Sandhills and a shingle spit, north of Deal, presumably enclosing marshy ground between the spit and the foot of the downs. The area now occupied by Deal and Walmer would probably have provided good beaches for drawing boats on to shore, though the seas can be treacherous off this area of the coast, with the sandbanks of the Goodwin Sands creating a hazard for shipping.

The presence of a masonry building at Downlands adds to a small group of buildings known from the east coast of Kent between the ports of Richborough and Dover. In 1922 a Roman building, presumed to be a villa, was excavated at Hull Place, Sholden, c 3km to the north-west of Downlands, (VCH Vol iii 1932, 152). Although no plan has been published, the building is described as having concrete foundations and frescoes. Another villa was discovered on the Sandwich by-pass in 1978, c 9km north-west of Downlands and c 2.5 km south of Richborough (Bennett 1978). The modest building appears to have consisted of a range of three rooms, those at the end projecting forward of the central room, fronted by a passage or verandah. The occupation of the building was dated to between AD 200 and 300. A third building, excavated in 1925, was discovered at Worth, c 8km to the

north-west of Downlands (Klein 1928). The foundations consisted of two concentric squares, with an outer dimension of around 16m, suggesting a Romano-Celtic temple. Dating evidence from its foundations suggested the building to belong to the mid fourth century or thereabouts.

The Sholden villa and Worth temple sit on a north-west to south-east ridge of high ground separated from the body of the North Downs by a system of valleys cutting across the axis of the dip slope and feeding into the Lydden valley, which cuts through the ridge c 5km north-west of Downlands. The Sholden villa lies to the southern shoulder of the Lydden valley, the temple to its north while Downlands lies above a valley feeding into it from the south. All three sites overlooked the coastal margin.

The position of the Downlands and Sholden 'villas' and the temple at Worth are perhaps significant given the discovery of the prestigious late Iron Age cemetery at Mill Hill, Deal (Parfitt 1995a). As has already been suggested this site indicates the presence of an important late Iron Age settlement based around the Lydden valley area. Although there is no evidence for late Iron Age origins to the settlements represented by these buildings it is tempting to suggest that their presence at least indicates continuity with the late Iron Age and that the Roman pattern of settlement, suggested as owing its origins to the late Iron Age, may extend at least as far as Walmer on the east coast of Kent.

The existence of these sites along the coastal margin, well away from the main route between Richborough and Dover, may indicate the presence of a subsidiary coastal route roughly following the line of the modern road from Sandwich to Deal and from Deal to Dover. The modern route of the Sandwich to Deal road extends from close to the Sandwich villa along the low ridge past the Worth temple, across the mouth of the Lydden valley and passes the site of the Sholden villa before dropping into Deal. From Deal the road changes direction climbing onto the downs, passing close to Downlands, and heading towards Dover. A road following this route would also have provided land access to St Margaret's Bay, with its sheltered beach. At its north end the suggested route may have turned east towards Woodnesborough, following Margary's route 101 (1955, 33) where it would have rejoined the main route.

The extent of settlement around Downlands in the late Iron Age and Roman periods is hinted at by a number of burials reported from the area. Some 400m to the south-east a Roman vessel and fragments of other urns were recovered from a gravel pit at Knights Bottom (Payne 1915, 283) and 600m further south a 'Belgic' bi-conical bowl was discovered in 1909 (SMR TR 34 NE 17), both finds presumably coming from cremations. About 900m to the north-east of Downlands late Iron Age and early Roman pottery, along with a pewter vessel and saucer, were found in 1886 at the site of St Mildred's Church, now demolished (Woodruff 1904, 14). These have been interpreted as indicating the presence of a cemetery and two skeletons found associated with late Iron Age or early Roman pottery, 150m south-west of this site, are suggested to belong to the same complex (Payne 1915,

283). At Walmer station *c* 1km to the north of Downlands Stebbing noted the discovery of Roman finds and elsewhere of graves in the railway cutting (SMR TR 35 SE 57).

Further evidence of late Iron Age and Roman occupation of the area comes from metal detecting finds from the fields to the south of Walmer. Coins of the first century BC have been found in several locations (SMR TR 34 NE 77 and 80, and SMR TR 35 SE 21). A metal detecting rally on land belonging to Walmer Court Farm in 1991 produced a late Iron Age coin and 142 Roman coins, ranging across the entire period, but mostly of fourth-century date (SMR TR 34 NE 112). A further late Iron Age coin and eleven Roman coins were recovered during a rally at Hawkshill Down in 1992 (SMR TR 34 NE 120) and another fifteen at a second location on Hawkshill Down in the same year, presumably at the same rally (SMR TR 34 NE 121).

Limited fieldwork, mostly watching brief and evaluation, has produced further evidence of late Iron Age and Romano-British occupation in the vicinity and some of the cropmarks discussed with the prehistoric period may be of a later date. The late Iron Age cemetery site at Mill Hill also produced evidence for Roman field boundary ditches. A watching brief on a water main adjacent to the A258 (Dover Road), 600m to the south of Downlands, produced two pits of Roman date (Parfitt 1981) and evaluation trenching at Hillcrest Gardens, Mill Hill, Deal, just under 1km to the north-west, revealed a pit and four gullies one of which produced a sherd of late Iron Age or early Roman date, along with Neolithic material (Parfitt 2001). Parfitt's survey of the archaeology of the Sandhills has demonstrated fairly extensive activity in the area to the north of Deal, including at least one settlement (Parfitt 1982).

This brief, and far from exhaustive, survey of the known sites in the landscape immediately around Downlands suggests widespread occupation of the area from the late Iron Age onwards. The extent and nature of this occupation remains unclear as there has been very little work done on the North Downs here, or to the west, and the majority of the known sites come from accidental finds from an agricultural landscape in which little development has occurred. Where roads and pipe schemes have cut through the downs there is increasing evidence of activity in these periods. It is therefore difficult to draw conclusions about the nature of any settlement in the hinterland to the west of the site and thus difficult to relate the site to any pattern of settlement pertaining to the downs. As stated above the results of Perkins' survey of the Romano-British settlement pattern of Thanet (Perkins 2001) suggests that the settlement density of Kent may be greater than the published evidence has previously suggested and indicates that many more sites remain to be found.

The chronology of the Roman settlement

The Roman occupation of the site is dated on the basis of a relatively small assemblage of pottery. Surprisingly, no coins were recovered from the site and with the exception of the late Iron Age brooch, no small finds were recovered which could contribute to the dating. The presence of the brooch is only of limited value in dating the site, as it could have remained in use for some time.

The larger part of the pottery assemblage was of second- or early to mid third-century date, with a smaller quantity of early material and very few late sherds. However some of the pottery styles present have a very long lifespan and cannot be dated with precision. The pottery recovered from the earlier Roman features on the site is reasonably fresh, suggesting primary deposition, and indicating they belong to the first or second centuries. The middle Roman material and earlier pottery recovered alongside it was generally in very poor condition and appears to have been lying exposed for some time prior to being cleared into this area. The bulk of this material was recovered from the redeposited soil horizon and deposits predating the building. A small quantity of late Roman pottery was also recovered from the soil horizon; this is in much better condition and is thought likely to have been intrusive.

The pottery assemblage produced no clearly late Iron Age ceramics and none of the native 'Belgic' pottery types need necessarily predate the Roman conquest. The evidence suggests that settlement of the area began in the first century AD, probably some time after AD 43, but no precision can be achieved. Occupation continued throughout the second and third centuries, but there is little evidence of fourth-century activity. The small quantity of fourth-century material and early Anglo-Saxon material recovered is insufficient to allow any conclusion about the presence of settlement on the site towards the latter part of the Roman and into the post-Roman periods. The absence of pottery directly associable with the building makes dating its construction difficult, but the dating of the pottery from the soil horizon suggests an early to mid third-century date, with the caveat that this material is redeposited. The absence of layers associated with its abandonment means that no end date for occupation can be given.

The nature of settlement at Downlands and the presence of the aisled building

The location of the excavation on the edge of the settled area at Downlands means that little can be said about the nature of the site in the early Roman period. Although the pottery assemblage does not suggest a particularly high status, the construction of an aisled building in the early to mid third century suggests that at least by this period the site had become relatively prosperous and was probably the site of a villa.

Aisled or basilican Roman buildings have been identified across much of the south of Britain, where they commonly form part of a larger complex of buildings. In Kent three aisled buildings have been identified at Darenth villa and others are known at Hartlip and Wilmington. More recent excavations have exposed aisled buildings at the Mount, Maidstone (Houliston 1999), Thurnham villa, near Maidstone, on the Channel Tunnel Rail Link (Oxford Archaeological Unit 2000b; 2001b) and c 8.5km to its southeast at Glebeland, Harrietsham, where nine buildings were identified, in at least two phases (Jarman 2002). At Thurnham a second, later structure may also have formed an aisled building, though the evidence is not conclusive.

The nature of aisled buildings has been the subject of some discussion (Collingwood 1930, 129–34; Smith 1963; Hadman 1978; King 1996, 66–9). The style of building has often been reconstructed on the basilican model with a nave lit by clerestory windows flanked by aisles - clearly taking its influence from classical architecture. Smith, looking at aisled barns, hall houses and long-houses from the medieval period, has suggested that the Roman buildings may have been spanned by a single roof and have more in common with these buildings than with the *basilica* of the Roman world. This view has become widely accepted in recent discussions. However, the discovery of the collapsed gable end façade at Meonstoke, Hampshire, provides clear evidence that this building was basilican in style and by inference that others were too (King 1996, 67). As King notes, this does not imply that all such buildings were basilican and structures such as the aisled buildings at Harrietsham (Jarman 2002), built on shallow, narrow and roughly-constructed flint footings with earthfast or pad supported aisle posts, suggest a timber frame supporting a single span roof.

The function of aisled buildings is unclear and they have been variously interpreted as villas or barns. Smith has suggested that, as with the medieval long-house, one end of the structure may have served an agricultural purpose, while the other end provided dwelling space (Smith 1963, 25–7). This interpretation appears to be supported by the excavation of an aisled building at West Blatchington, Hove (Norris and Burstow 1950), where the northern end of the building was divided into rooms and the south end left open. At Meonstoke, where only the south-east end of the building was excavated, the insertion of a hypocaust again indicated occupation (King 1996, 58), though the author points out that the building possibly was of mixed function (*ibid*, 67). Elsewhere, interpretation is more commonly purely agricultural buildings. At the Mount, Maidstone, the aisled building was interpreted as a barn or byre (Houliston 1999, 161); at Thurnham a corn-drying oven was present within the main aisled building indicating it to be agricultural and a second, possible aisled structure was also interpreted as agricultural (Oxford Archaeological Unit 2001b, 15–16).

It is probable that we are in fact looking at two separate types of construction and possibly differences in function. The more substantially built aisled buildings often with pier bases of stone suggesting an arcade supporting a clerestory, such as that reconstructed for Meonstoke (King 1996), may be basilican. These grander structures may be suggested to form accommodation, at least in part, though they may simply be an indication of status, creating a grand appearance to the building complex, and rooms could have been offices, separate stores or stabling. The less substantial buildings, such as those at Harrietsham using earthfast posts,

are more likely to represent agricultural buildings, closer in appearance to the medieval barn, though the possibility that they were used as dwellings cannot be precluded.

The aisled building at Thurnham probably presents the best local structure comparable to that at Downlands and its size and construction are very similar. The Thurnham example was 21m long by 14m wide, with six pairs of aisle posts forming a 6m wide nave and 3m wide aisles. The outer walls of the building were formed by shallow loosely mortared flint footings, around 1m wide, and the roof was supported by substantial aisle posts. The building was located c 50m to the east of the main villa building on a roughly perpendicular alignment. Some 40m to its south lay a shrine or temple. Other structures and enclosures were observed around this main complex, including a second possible aisled building.

The arrangement and types of buildings present at Thurnham have been observed at several other sites and appear to form a fairly common layout in the later second and third centuries. By analogy with Thurnham, and other sites, it is suggested that the Downlands building may be an ancillary building accompanying a separate villa building and possibly other structures. If we are to accept the layout of Thurnham as typical then the main building can be expected to lie to the south of the excavation area, further up the slope and to face north-east, taking in the commanding view across the Wantsum channel towards the Isle of Thanet.

The substantial nature of both the Downlands and Thurnham buildings suggests quite grand structures. The outer wall foundations of both buildings appear too wide and, at Downlands at least, too substantial to have supported an entirely timber-framed superstructure. It is therefore suggested that the building at Downlands had masonry walls up to eaves level and probably at the gable ends. However the usage of earthfast posts to support the roof suggests a single span roof rather than a clerestory, suggesting the structure to be aisled rather than basilican.

The suggested dating of the aisled building at Downlands to the third century is paralleled at a number of other sites, eg Meonstoke (King 1996, 56), West Blatchington (Norris and Burstow 1950) and Harrietsham (Jarman 2002), while those at the Mount (Houliston 1999, 161), Thurnham (Oxford Archaeological Unit, 2000a; 2001b) and building K at Darenth (Detsicas 1987, 107) may be slightly earlier, dating to the mid or later part of the second century.

The economy of Downlands in the Roman period

Evidence for the economy of Downlands is limited. The pottery recovered contributes little to our understanding. The assemblage is entirely typical of domestic usage, with little evidence for imports or specific function, and across the entire duration of the occupation suggests little variation in economic status. The minimal assemblage of small finds, with few iron or other metal artefacts, is similarly unhelpful and the absence of coins is of note.

The quantities of animal bone and plant remains recovered are very small and allow only limited conclusions. The presence of animal bone in such small quantities need not imply anything more than domestic consumption. In general the quantity of charred plant remains recovered was low and, as has been noted elsewhere, the problems of cross-contamination between phases is high. However samples taken from two deposits, one associated with the construction of the aisled building and the other from the backfill of the associated ditch are significant. Both deposits produced large quantities of cereal grain and chaff, indicating the processing of cereal crops (*see* p 74). The presence of fragments of quernstone give added support to this suggestion. As in the prehistoric period the principal crops present were spelt wheat and hulled barley. Ruth Pelling notes that the quantity of weed seeds in the samples is low and suggests that this results from sorting prior to storage and processing. This she suggests is labour intensive, suggesting a large, seasonal labour force sufficient to carry out this task before storing the grain. She further suggests that this would be expected of a site large enough to support one or more grain drying ovens. This suggestion would support the conclusion that the aisled building formed part of a villa complex. Although the relationship of these deposits with the aisled building is not certain, it seems reasonable to assume that they do reflect the economic activity associated with the building and the site in general in its later phases. Of note within one sample was the presence of sprouted wheat seeds apparently derived from the malting process. If correct this may indicate that brewing of wheat beer was taking place at the site, a suggestion paralleled at other sites (*see* p 74).

Recovery of weed seeds from sampling was limited, but as with the prehistoric period suggested weeds of cereal crops and open, disturbed ground. The weed seeds derived from the samples were indicative of cultivation of lighter soils with no indication of cultivation of the heavier clay soils or chalky soils. This may indicate that the cereal was brought in from some distance, but is more likely to indicate that cereal growing was concentrated on the lighter silts found within the dry valleys cutting off the downs to either side of the site. The more chalky areas and those with heavy clay-with-flint subsoil may have been used for grazing and wood coppicing respectively.

Given the proximity to the sea it is surprising that very little shellfish was recovered, suggesting only limited utilisation of the resources that it provided. Only one pit produced a significant quantity of shellfish and the incidence of fish bones in samples was very low; the latter may be in part due to poor preservation in unfavourable soil conditions. The pit containing shellfish suggests a wide range to have been eaten, including oyster, mussels, winkle and limpet. The ubiquitous oyster shells found across so many sites were not present in great number at Downlands.

Evidence for other economic activities was non-existent and with so little of the site having been investigated it is unwise to suggest too much about its nature. The aisled building is suggested by analogy with other sites to be a barn, but such a building could equally have served other commercial or domestic functions, its presence and form being a matter of taste or fashion as much as function.

The absence of coins from the site is surprising and this, in combination with the nature of the pottery assemblage would, if it were not for the presence of the aisled building, suggest nothing more than a typical farmstead or small settlement. However as has been discussed above, the substantial building, possibly with masonry walls, suggests a higher status to the site, perhaps even indicating the presence of a villa, albeit a modest one.

6
Bibliography

Allen, T, Parfitt, K and Rady, J 1997, 'Thanet Way', *Canterbury's Archaeology 1995–1996*, 24–7

Amorosi, T 1989, '*A Postcranial Guide to Domestic Neo-Natal and Juvenile Mammals*', British Archaeological Reports (International Series) 533, Oxford

Andrews, C 2001, 'Romanisation: a Kentish perspective', *Archaeologia Cantiana* cxxi, 25–42

Arnold, D 1985, *Ceramic Theory and Cultural Process*, Cambridge

Arthur, P 1986, 'Roman Amphorae from Canterbury', *Britannia* xvii, 239–58

Aufderheide, A and Rodríguez-Martín, C 1998, *The Cambridge Encyclopedia of Human Palaepathology*, Cambridge

Baker, B 1999, 'Early manifestations of tuberculosis in the skeleton' in G Pálfi, O Dutour, J Deák and I Hutás, *Tuberculosis Past and Present*, Budapest, 301–7

Baker, J and Brothwell, D 1980, *Animal Diseases in Archaeology*, London

Barrett, J 1980, 'The pottery of the Later Bronze Age in Lowland England', *Proceedings of the Prehistoric Society* 46, 297–319

Bathurst, R and Barta, J 2004, 'Molecular evidence of tuberculosis induced hypertrophic osteopathy in a 16th-century Iroquoian dog', *Journal of Archaeological Science* 31, 917–25

Bendrey, R 2002, 'Roman mammalian remains' in R Taylor-Wilson, *Excavations at Hunt's House, Guy's Hospital, London Borough of Southwark*, Pre-Construct Archaeology Limited, Monograph No 1, 57–60

Bendrey, R 2007a, 'The development of new methodologies for studying the horse: case studies from prehistoric southern England', unpublished PhD thesis, University of Southampton

Bendrey, R 2007b, 'New methods for the identification of evidence for bitting on horse remains from archaeological sites', *Journal of Archaeological Science* 34, 1036–50

Bendrey, R 2008, 'A possible case of tuberculosis or brucellosis in an Iron Age horse skeleton from Viables Farm, Basingstoke, England' in Z Miklikova and R Thomas (eds), *Current Research in Animal Palaeopathology: Proceedings of the Second Animal Palaeopathology Working Group Conference*, British Archaeological Reports (International Series) 1844, 19–26

Bennett, P 1978, 'A Roman building near Sandwich', *Archaeologia Cantiana* xciv, 191–4

Bennett, P, Frere, S S and Stow, S 1982, *Excavations at Canterbury Castle*, The Archaeology of Canterbury I, Maidstone

Bennett, P, Couldrey, P and Macpherson-Grant, N 2007, *Highstead near Chislet, Kent. Excavations 1975–77*, The Archaeology of Canterbury, New Series, IV, Canterbury

Bevan, L forthcoming, 'A Late Bronze Age flint assemblage from the riverside zone at Runnymede Bridge, Egham, Surrey', British Museum monograph

Blagg, T 1982, 'Roman Kent' in P Leach (ed), 51–60

Blanquaert, G and Bostyn, F 1998, 'L'âge du fer à Coquelles et Fréthun (Pas de Calais) (Fouilles du Transmanche 1986–1988)', *Revue du Nord 80*, 109–37

Blockley, K, Blockley, M, Blockley, P, Frere, S S and Stow, S 1995, *Excavations in the Marlowe Car Park and Surrounding Areas*, The Archaeology of Canterbury V, Canterbury

Blurton, T 1977, 'Excavations at Angel Court, Walbrook, 1974', *Transactions of the London and Middlesex Archaeological Society* 28, 14–100

Boessneck, J 1969, 'Osteological differences between sheep (*Ovis aries* Linné) and goat (*Capra hircus* Linné)' in D Brothwell and E Higgs (eds), *Science in Archaeology*, London, 331–58

Booth, P 2001, 'The Roman shrine at Westhawk Farm, Ashford: a preliminary account', *Archaeologia Cantiana* cxxi, 1–24

Bond, D 1988, *Excavation at the North ring, Mucking, Essex: A late Bronze Age Enclosure*, East Anglian Archaeological Monograph 43, Gressenhall

Bradley, R and Ellison, A 1975, *Rams Hill*, British Archaeological Reports (British Series) 19, Oxford

British Geological Survey, 1:50,000 Series, Dover, Sheet 290

Brown, L 2000, 'The later prehistoric pottery' in B Cunliffe, *The Danebury environs programme; The prehistory of a Wessex Landscape Volume 1*, 79–127, Oxford

Brown, N 1988, 'A Late Bronze Age enclosure at Lofts Farm, Essex', *Proceedings of the Prehistoric Society* 54, 248–302

Brown, N 1995a, 'Later Bronze Age to Early Iron Age pottery' in J J Wymer, and N R Brown, *Excavations at North Shoebury: settlement and economy in southeast Essex 1500 BC–AD 1500*, East Anglian Archaeology Report No 75, 77–88

Brown, N 1995b, 'Prehistoric pottery' in J Ecclestone, 'Early Iron Age settlement at Southend: excavations at Fox Hall Farm, 1993', *Essex Archaeology and History* 26, 28–35

Brück, J 1999, 'Houses, lifecycles, and deposition on Middle Bronze Age settlements in southern England', *Proceedings of the Prehistoric Society* 65, 145–66

Brück, J 2007, 'The character of Late Bronze Age settlement in southern Britain' in C Haselgrove and R Pope, *The Earlier Iron Age in Britain and the near Continent*, Oxford, 24–38

Bryan, E 2002, *Iron Age pottery from Dumpton Gap, Broadstairs* unpublished MA dissertation, University of Southampton

Bryan, E 2006, 'Later prehistoric pottery from Little Stock Farm' in K Ritchie, *The prehistoric settlement at Little Stock Farm, Mersham, Kent*, CTRL integrated site report series, ADS 2006

Buckley, D and Hedges, J 1987, *The Bronze Age and Saxon Settlements at Springfield Lyons, Essex: An interim report*, Essex County Council Occasional Paper 5, Chelmsford

Butler, C 2005, *Prehistoric Flintwork*, Stroud

Campbell, G 2008, 'Charred plant remains' in B Cunliffe and C Poole, *The Danebury Environs Roman Programme: A Wessex landscape in the Roman era, Volume 2, Part 2: Grateley South, Grateley, Hants 1998 and 1999*, English Heritage and Oxford University School of Archaeology Monograph 71, 166–74

Champion, T 1980, 'Settlement and environment in Later Bronze Age Kent' in J Barrett and R Bradley (eds), *The British Later Bronze Age*, British Archaeological Reports (British Series) 83, parts i and ii, Oxford, 223–46

Champion, T 1982, 'The Bronze Age in Kent' in P Leach (ed), 31–9

Champion, T 2007a, 'Settlement in Kent from 1500 to 300 BC' in C Haselgrove and R Pope, *The Earlier Iron Age in Britain and the near Continent*, Oxford, 293–305

Champion, T 2007b, 'The importance of Highstead' in P Bennett *et al*, 2007, 283–94

Clapham, A, Tutin, T and Moore, D 1989, *Flora of the British Isles* (3rd edition), Cambridge University Press

Cleal, R 1995, 'Pottery fabrics in Wessex in the fourth to second millennia BC' in I Kinnes and G Varndell (eds), *Unbaked urns of rudely shape*, Oxford, 185–95

Collingwood, R G 1930, *The Archaeology of Roman Britain*, London

Cornevin, C and Lesbre, X 1894, *Traité de l'age des animaux domestiques: d'après les dents et les productions épidermiques*, Paris

Cotton, J 2002, 'The Lithics' in J Sidell, J Cotton and L Rayner, *The Prehistory of Southwark and Lambeth*, MoLAS Monograph 14, London, 68–88

Couldrey, P 2007, 'Continental influence' in P Bennett *et al*, 167–70

Crummy, N 1983, *The Roman Small Finds from Excavations in Colchester 1971–9*, Colchester Archaeological Reports 2, Colchester

Cunliffe, B 1982, 'Social and economic development in Kent in the pre-Roman Iron Age' in P Leach (ed), 40–50

Cunliffe, B 1991a, *Danebury: An Iron Age Hillfort in Hampshire. Volume 4. The excavations 1979–1988: the Site*, Council for British Archaeology Research Report 73, York

Cunliffe, B 1991b, *Iron Age communities in Britain*, third edition, London and New York

Cunliffe, B 1995, *Danebury: An Iron Age Hillfort in Hampshire. Volume 6. A hillfort community in perspective*, Council for British Archaeology Research Report 102, York

Detsicas, A 1983, *The Cantiaci*, Gloucester

Detsicas, A 1966, 'An Iron Age and Romano-British site at Stone Castle Quarry, Greenhithe', *Archaeologia Cantiana* lxxxi, 136–90

Diack, M 2003, 'North Foreland Road, Broadstairs, *Canterbury's Archaeology 2000–2001*, 25–6

Dines, H G, Holmes, S C A and Robbie, J A 1954, *Geology of the Country around Chatham*, London

Dobney, K and Rielly, K 1988, 'A method for recording archaeological animal bones: the use of diagnostic zones', *Circaea* 5.1, 79–96

von den Driesch, A 1976, *A Guide to the Measurement of Animal Bones from Archaeological Sites*, Peabody Museum Bulletin 1, Cambridge, Massachusetts

Edmonds, M 1995, *Stone Tools and Society*, London

Gallagher, J 1977, 'Contemporary Stone Tools in Ethiopia', *Journal of Field Archaeology*, Vol 4, 407–14

Gibson, A 2002, *Prehistoric Pottery in Britain and Ireland*, Gloucester

Grant, A 1984, 'Survival or Sacrifice? A critical appraisal of animal bones in Britain in the Iron Age' in C Grigson and S Payne (eds), *Ageing and Sexing Animal Bones from Archaeological Sites*, British Archaeological Reports (British Series) 109, Oxford, 91–108

Grigson, C and Clutton-Brock, J 1984 (eds), *Animals and Archaeology: 4. Husbandry in Europe*, British Archaeological Reports (International Series) 227, Oxford

Guttman, E and Last, J 2000, 'A Late Bronze Age landscape at Hornchurch, Essex', *Proceedings of the Prehistoric Society* 66, 319–59

Hadman, J 1978, 'Aisled Buildings in Roman Britain', in M Todd, *Studies in the Romano-British Villa*, Leicester, 187–95

Halstead, P 1985, 'A study of mandibular teeth from Romano-British contexts at Maxey' in F Pryor, C French, D Crowther, D Gurney, G Simpson and M Taylor (eds), *Archaeology and Environment in the Lower Welland Valley Volume 1*, East Anglian Archaeology Report 27, 219–24

Hambleton, E 1999, *Animal Husbandry Regimes in Iron Age Britain: a comparative study of faunal assemblages from British Iron Age sites*, British Archaeological Reports (British Series) 282, Oxford

Hamilton, S 1987, 'Late Bronze Age pottery' in D Rudling, 'The excavation of a Late Bronze Age site at Yapton, West Sussex', *Sussex Archaeological Collections* 125, 51–67

Hamilton, S 1988, 'Earlier first millennium BC pottery from Rectory Road and Baker Street' in T Wilkinson, *Archaeology and Environment in South Essex: Rescue archaeology along the Grays By-pass 1979/80*, East Anglian Archaeology Report No 42, 77–86

Hamilton, S 2001, 'A review of the early first millennium BC pottery from Chanctonbury Ring: a contribution to the study of Sussex hillforts of the Late Bronze Age/Early Iron Age transition' in D Rudling, 'Chanctonbury Ring revisited, the excavations of 1988–91', *Sussex Archaeological Collections* 139, 75–121

Harcourt, R 1974, 'The dog in prehistoric and early historic Britain', *Journal of Archaeological Science* 1, 151–76

Hartley, K 1982, 'The Mortaria', in P Bennettt *et al*, 150–8

Haselgrove, C and Pope, R 2007, 'Characterising the earlier Iron Age' in *The Earlier Iron Age in Britain and the near continent*, Oxford, 1–24

Hasted, E 1798, *History of Kent*, Vol IX, 565

Hattatt, R 1989, *A Visual Catalogue of Richard Hattatt's Ancient Brooches*, Oxford

Hatting, T 1975, 'The influence of castration on sheep horns' in A Clason (ed), *Archaeozoological studies*, Elsevier, 345–51

Hawkes, C and Hull, M 1947, *Camulodunum: first report on the excavations at Colchester, 1930–1939*, Reports of the Research Committee of the Society of Antiquaries of London XIV, Oxford

Heritage Conservation Group 2005, *Specification for a programme of archaeological investigation in advance of the construction of residential development on land at Downlands, Walmer, Kent*

Hearne, C, Perkins, D and Andrews, P 1995, 'The Sandwich Bay wastewater treatment scheme archaeological project', *Archaeologia Cantiana* cxv, 239–354

Herne, A 1991, 'The flint assemblage' in I Longworth, A Herne, G Varndell and S Needham, *Excavations at Grimes Graves, Norfolk 1972–76*, Fascicule 3, British Museum Press, 21–93

Hill, J 1995, *Ritual and rubbish in the Iron Age of Wessex*, British Archaeological Reports (British Series) 242, Oxford

Hillison, S 1996, *Dental Anthropology*, Cambridge

Hinton, P 1982, 'Carbonised seeds', 382–90 in P Drewett, 'Later Bronze Age downland economy and excavations at Black Patch, East Sussex', *Proceedings of the Prehistoric Society* 48, 321–400

Houliston, M 1999, 'Excavations at the Mount Roman villa, Maidstone, 1994', *Archaeologia Cantiana* cxix, 71–172

Humphrey, J and Young, R 2003, 'Flint use in Later Bronze and Iron Age England? Some criteria for future research' in N Moloney and M Shott (eds), *Lithic Analysis at the Millennium*, London, 79–89

Hurd, H 1909, 'On a Late Celtic village near Dumpton Gap, Broadstairs', *Archaeologia Cantiana* lxi, 427–8

Ingrem, C and Clark, K 2005, 'Horse burials and a dog burial' in J Hiller and D Wilkinson, *Archaeology of the Jubilee Line Extension: Prehistoric and Roman activity at Stratford Market Depot, West Ham, London 1991–1993*, Museum of London Archaeology Service, 40–4

Jarman, C 2002, 'Glebe Land, Marley Road, Harrietsham', *Canterbury's Archaeology 1997–1998*, 16–17

Jarman, C 2003, 'Archaeological evaluation on land at Downlands, Walmer, near Deal, Kent: Interim Report', unpublished Canterbury Archaeological Trust report, 2003/142

Jarman, C 2004, 'Archaeological evaluation on land at Downlands, Walmer, near Deal, Kent', unpublished Canterbury Archaeological Trust report, 2004/78

Jarman, C 2005, 'Underdown Lane, Eddington', *Canterbury's Archaeology 2003–2004*, 14–16

Jarman, C 2006, *Archaeological excavation on land at Downlands, Walmer, near Deal, Kent: Stratigraphic assessment report*, unpublished Canterbury Archaeological Trust report, 2006/6

Jarman, C and Shand, G 2003, *Excavation of a multi-period site at Eddington, near Herne Bay, Kent, 1999–2000*, unpublished Canterbury Archaeological Trust client report, 2003/37

Jones, G 2006a, 'Later prehistoric pottery from Saltwood Tunnel' in I Riddler and M Trevarthen, *The prehistoric, Roman and Anglo-Saxon funerary landscape at Saltwood Tunnel, Kent, CTRL integrated site report series* in ADS 2006

Jones, G 2006b, 'Later prehistoric pottery from Beechbrook Wood' in I Riddler, and M Trevarthen, *The prehistoric, Roman and Anglo-Saxon funerary landscape at Saltwood Tunnel, Kent, CTRL integrated site report series* in ADS 2006

Jones, M and Bond, D 1980, 'Later Bronze Age settlement at Mucking, Essex,' in J Barrett and R Bradley (eds), *The British Later Bronze Age*, British Archaeological Reports (British Series) 83, 471–82

Kiesewalter, L 1888, *Skelettmessungen an Pferden als Beitrag zur theoretischen Grundlage der Beurteilungslehre des Pferdes*, dissertation, Leipzig

King, A 1996, 'The south-east façade of Meonstoke aisled building' in P Johnson (ed), *Architecture in Roman Britain*, Council for British Archaeology Research Report 94, 56–69

Klein, L 1928, 'Roman temple at Worth, Kent', *Antiquaries Journal* viii, 76–86

Knight, S 2001, 'Beasts and burial in the interpretation of ritual space: a case study from Danebury' in A Smith and A Brookes (eds), *Holy Ground: Theoretical Issues Relating to the Landscape and Material Culture of Ritual Space Objects*, British Archaeological Reports (International Series) 956, Oxford, 49–50

Leach, P 1982 (ed), *Archaeology in Kent to AD 1500*, Council for British Archaeology Research Report 48, London

Levine, M 1982, 'The use of crown height measurements and eruption-wear sequences to age horse teeth' in B Wilson, C Grigson and S Payne (eds) *Ageing and Sexing Animal Bones from Archaeological Sites*, British Archaeological Reports (British Series) 109, Oxford, 223–350

Levine, M, Whitwell, K and Jeffcott, L 2002, 'A Romano-British horse burial from Icklingham, Suffolk', *Archaeofauna* 11, 63–102

Ligncreux, Y and Peters, J 1999, 'Elements for the retrospective diagnosis of tuberculosis on animal bones from archaeological sites' in G Pálfi, O Dutour, J Deák and I Hutás, *Tuberculosis Past and Present*, Budapest, 339–48

Longley, D 1980, *Runnymede Bridge 1976: Excavations on the site of a Late Bronze Age Settlement,* Surrey Archaeological Society Research Volume No 6, Guildford

Macpherson-Grant, N 1980, 'Archaeological work along the A2, 1966–74', *Archaeologia Cantiana* xcvi, 133–83

Macpherson-Grant, N 1990, 'The pottery from the 1987–1989 Channel Tunnel Excavations', *Canterbury's Archaeology 1988–1989,* 60–3

Macpherson-Grant, N 1991, 'A Re-appraisal of prehistoric pottery from Canterbury', *Canterbury's Archaeology 1990–1991,* 38–48

Macpherson-Grant, N 1992, 'Appendix 11: The pottery' in D Perkins, 'Archaeological evaluations at Ebbsfleet in the Isle of Thanet', *Archaeologia Cantiana* cxii, 286–303

Macpherson-Grant, N 1997, 'The ceramics from Whitfield-Eastry by-pass Site 2', *Canterbury's Archaeology 1995–1996,* 67–8

Manning, W 1985, *Catalogue of the Romano-British Iron Tools, Fittings and Weapons in the British Museum*, London

Margary, I 1955, *Roman roads in Britain*, London

Martin-Kilcher, S 1983, 'Les amphores romaines a huile de Betique (Dressel 20 et 23) d'Augst (Colonia Augusta Rauricorum) et Kaiseraugst (Castrum Rauracense). Un rapport preliminaire' in J Blazquez and J Remsedal (eds), *Prod. Y Com. del. Aceite en la Antiguedad. II Congresso*, Madrid, 337–47

Mays, S 1998, *The Archaeology of Human Bones*, London

McNee, B 2006, 'Chalk Hill, Ramsgate Harbour Approach Road. Later Prehistoric Pottery', unpublished Canterbury Archaeological Trust archive report

McNee, B 2007, 'Prehistoric pottery from Ellington School, Pysons Road, Ramsgate, Kent', unpublished Canterbury Archaeological Trust report

McNee, B forthcoming, 'Later Prehistoric Pottery' in P Clark, G Shand and J Weekes, 'Excavations at Chalk Hill, Ramsgate, Kent, 1997–98', Canterbury Archaeological Trust Occasional Paper

Middleton, A 1995, 'Prehistoric red-finished pottery from Kent' in I Kinnes and G Varndell (eds), *Unbaked urns of rudely shape,* Oxford, 203–11

Millett, M 2007, 'Roman Kent' in J Williams (ed), *The Archaeology of Kent to AD 800*, Kent County Council, Maidstone

Moffett, L 1986, *Crops and crop processing in a Romano-British Village at Tiddington: The evidence from the charred plant remains*, Ancient Monuments Laboratory Report 15/86

Monaghan, J 1987, *Upchurch and Thameside Roman Pottery*, British Archaeological Reports (British Series) 173, Oxford

Morris, E 1994a, 'Production and distribution of pottery and salt in Iron Age Wessex: a review', *Proceedings of the Prehistoric Society* 60, 371–94

Morris, E 1994b, 'The organisation of pottery production and distribution in Iron Age Wessex' in A Patrick and E Morris (eds), *The Iron Age in Wessex: recent works,* Salisbury, 26–9

Morris, E 2006, 'Later prehistoric pottery from White Horse Stone' in P Booth (ed), *Ceramics from Section 1 of the Channel Tunnel Rail Link, Kent*, CTRL scheme-wide specialist report series in ADS 2006

Norris, N and Burstow, G 1950, 'A prehistoric and Romano-British site at West Blatchington, Hove', *Sussex Archaeological Collections* 89, 1–56

O'Connor, T 1985, 'On quantifying vertebrates: some sceptical observations', *Circaea* 3, 27–30

Ogilvie, J 1977, 'The Stourmouth–Adisham water main trench' *Archaeologia Cantiana* xciii, 91–124

Orton, C 1977, 'Introduction to the pottery reports' in T Blurton, 28–30

Outram, A 2001, 'A new approach to identifying bone marrow and grease exploitation: why the "indeterminate" fragments should not be ignored', *Journal of Archaeological Science* 28, 401–10

Oxford Archaeological Unit 2000a, 'White Horse Stone: a Neolithic longhouse', *Current Archaeology* 168, 450–53

Oxford Archaeological Unit 2000b, 'Thurnham Roman Villa', *Current Archaeology* 168, 454–7

Oxford Archaeological Unit 2001a, *White Horse Stone, Aylesford, Kent*, unpublished assessment report

Oxford Archaeological Unit 2001b, *Thurnham Roman Villa: Post-excavation assessment report*, unpublished assessment report

Parfitt, K 1981, 'The Ringwould water main, 1980/81', *Kent Archaeological Review* 65, 107–11

Parfitt, K 1982, 'Roman finds from the Sandhills, north of Deal', *Kent Archaeological Review* 70, 225–7

Parfitt, K 1993, 'Watching brief for new Deal reservoir: Phase 3, the pipelines', unpublished Canterbury Archaeological Trust client report

Parfitt, K 1995a, *Iron Age Burials from Mill Hill*, Deal, London

Parfitt, K 1995b, 'Herne Bay waste water pipeline', *Canterbury's Archaeology 1995–1996*, 32–3

Parfitt, K 1997, 'Watching brief at No 429 Dover Road, Walmer', unpublished Canterbury Archaeological Trust client report

Parfitt, K 2001, 'Watching brief off Hillcrest Gardens', unpublished Dover Archaeological Group report

Parfitt, K, Allen, T and Rady, J 1997, 'Whitfield-Eastry by-pass', *Canterbury's Archaeology 1995–1996*, 28–33

Payne, G 1915, 'Researches and discoveries in Kent', *Archaeologia Cantiana* xxxi, 283

Payne, S 1985, 'Morphological distinctions between the mandibular teeth of young sheep, *Ovis*, and goats, *Capra*', *Journal of Archaeological Science* 12, 139–47

Peacock, D 1977, 'Ceramics in Roman and Medieval Archaeology' in D Peacock (ed), *Pottery and Early Commerce*, London, 21–34

Peacock, D 1982, *Pottery in the Roman World: an ethnoarchaeological approach*, London

Peacock, D and Williams, D 1986, *Amphorae and the Roman economy: an introductory guide*, London

Pearson, E and Robinson, M 1994, 'Environmental evidence from the villa' in R Williams and R Zeepvat, *Bancroft: a late Bronze Age/ Iron Age settlement, Roman Villa and Temple-Mausoleum* (2 vols), Buckinghamshire Archaeological Society Monograph, Series 7, 565–84

Pelling, R 2000a, 'Charred plant remains', pp 324–8 in P Booth and C Hayden, 'A Roman Settlement at Mansfield College, Oxford', *Oxoniensia* 65, 291–331

Pelling, R 2000b, 'The Charred Plant Remains' in I Scott, 'Excavations on the site of the former Hockley Chemical Works, Stratford Road, Alcester, 1994', *Transactions of the Birmingham and Warwickshire Archaeological Society*, 104, 1–74

Pelling, R 2003, 'Charred Plant Remains', pp 71–4 in P Hutchings, 'Ritual and riverside settlement: a multi-period site at Princes Road, Dartford', *Archaeologia Cantiana* cxxiii, 41–79

Perkins, D 1995, 'Report on work by the Trust for Thanet Archaeology', *Archaeologia Cantiana* cxv, 468–78

Perkins, D 1996, 'The Trust for Thanet Archaeology: evaluation work carried out in 1995, Hartsdown Community Woodland Scheme', *Archaeologia Cantiana* cxvi, 265–81

Perkins, D 1997, 'Report on work by the Trust for Thanet Archaeology', *Archaeologia Cantiana* cxvii, 227

Perkins, D 2001, 'The Roman archaeology of the Isle of Thanet', *Archaeologia Cantiana* cxxi, 25–42

Perkins, D, Macpherson-Grant, N, Healey, E 1994, 'Monkton Court Farm evaluation', *Archaeologia Cantiana* cxiv, 237–316

Petrie, W 1880, 'Notes on Kentish earthworks', *Archaeologia Cantiana* xiii, 13

Philp, B 1984, *Excavations in the Darent Valley, Kent*, Dover, 8–72

Pitts, M 1978, 'On the shape of waste flakes as an index of technological change in lithic industries', *Journal of Archaeological Science* 5, 17–37

Pollard, R 1988, *The Roman Pottery of Kent*, Kent Archaeological Society Monograph, Vol V, Maidstone

Pollard, R 1995a, 'Pottery from the Augustan to the Vespasianic years' in K Blockley *et al*, 585–624

Pollard, R 1995b, 'The Mid to Late Roman period' in K Blockley *et al*, 690–736

Poole, C 1984, 'Objects of baked clay' in B Cunliffe, *Danebury: an Iron Age Hillfort in Hampshire,* Council for British Archaeology Research Report 2, London, 110–22

PPG 16 1990, *Planning and Archaeology: Policy Guidance Note 16*, English Heritage, London

Prehistoric Ceramics Research Group 1997, *The Study of Later Prehistoric Pottery: General policies and Guidelines for Analysis and Publication,* Prehistoric Ceramics Research Group, Occasional Papers Nos 1 and 2, Oxford

Pryor, F 1998, *Farmers in Prehistoric Britain*, Stroud

Rady, J 1995, 'Whitfield–Eastry improvement road: Report on trial trenching project north of Venson Road', unpublished Canterbury Archaeological Trust client report, 1995/24

Rady, J forthcoming, 'The Archaeology of the Channel Tunnel'

Rigby, V 1977, 'The Gallo-Belgic pottery from Cirencester' in J Dore and K Greene (eds), *Roman pottery studies in Britain and beyond*, British Archaeological Reports S30, Oxford, 37–45

Roberts, C and Manchester, K 1999, *The Archaeology of Disease*, (third edition), New York

Rooney, J 1997, 'Equid Palaeopathology', *Journal of Equine Veterinary Science* 17, 430–46

Saville, A 1981, *Grimes Graves, Norfolk. Excavations 1971–2: Volume II, the flint assemblage,* Department of the Environment Archaeological Research Report 11, London

Scheuer, L and Black, S 2004, *The Juvenile Skeleton*, Elsevier Academic Press

Schmid, E 1972, *Atlas of Animal Bones*, Amsterdam

Shand, G 2001a, *Archaeological Excavations at Chalk Hill, Ramsgate Harbour Approach Road 1997/8, Stratigraphic Report,* unpublished Canterbury Archaeological Trust report

Shand, G 2001b, 'Ramsgate Harbour Approach Road', *Canterbury's Archaeology 1998–1999,* 18–22

Shephard-Thorn, E 1988, *Geology of the county around Ramsgate and Dover,* London

Silver, I 1969, 'The ageing of domestic animals' in D Brothwell and E Higgs (eds), *Science and Archaeology*, London, 283–302

Sinipoli, C M 1991, *Approaches to Archaeological Ceramics*, New York and London

Skibo, J and Schiffer, M 1995, 'The clay cooking pot: an exploration of women's technology' in J Skibo, W Walker and A Nelson (eds), *Expanding Archaeology*, Salt Lake City, 80–91

Smith, J 1963, 'Romano-British aisled houses' *Archaeological Journal* cxx, 1–30

Stebbing, W P D 1934, 'An early Iron Age site at Deal', *Archaeologia Cantiana* xlvi, 207–9

Stevens, C 2003, 'An investigation of agricultural consumption and production models for prehistoric and Roman Britain', *Environmental Archaeology* 8, 61–76

Sunter, N and Woodward, P 1987, *Romano-British Industries in Purbeck, Dorchester*, Dorset Natural History and Archaeological Monograph No 6, Dorchester

Thompson, F 1983, 'Excavations at Bigbury, near Canterbury, 1978–80', *Antiquaries Journal* lxiii, 239–78

Thompson, I 1982, *Grog-tempered 'Belgic' pottery of South-Eastern England*, British Archaeological Reports (British Series) 108, Oxford

Tomber, M and Dore, J 1998, *The National Roman Fabric Reference Collection*, MoLAS Monograph 2, London

Turner, R and Wymer, J 1987, 'An assemblage of Palaeolithic handaxes from the Roman religious complex at Ivy Chimneys, Witham, Essex', *Antiquaries Journal* cxvii, 54–5

United Kingdom Institute for Conservation 1983, *Conservation Guidelines*, London

van der Veen, M 1989, 'Charred grain assemblages from Roman-period corn driers in Britain', *Archaeological Journal* 146, 302–19

van der Veen, M and Jones, G 2006, 'A re-analysis of agricultural production and consumption: implications for understanding the British Iron Age', *Vegetation History and Archaeobotany* 15 (3), 217–28

Victoria County History, 1932, Kent, Vol iii, 152

Webster, P 1993, *Roman Samian Pottery in Britain*, Council for British Archaeology Practical Handbook in Archaeology 13, York

White, T 2000, *Human Osteology,* second edition, London

Wilson, B 1992, 'Considerations for the identification of ritual deposits of animal bones in Iron Age pits', *International Journal of Osteoarchaeology* 2(4), 341–9

Woodruff, C 1904, 'Further discoveries of late Celtic and Romano-British interments at Walmer', *Archaeologia Cantiana* xxvi, 14

Wymer, J and Brown, N 1995, *Excavations at North Shoebury:settlement and economy in south-east Essex 1500 BC – AD 1500*, Chelmsford

Yates, D 2001, 'Bronze Age agricultural intensification in the Thames Valley and Estuary' in J Brück (ed), *Bronze Age Landscapes: transition and transformation*, Oxford, 65–82

Young, R and Humphrey, J 1999, 'Flint use in Later Bronze Age and Iron Age England – fact or fiction?', *Lithics* 20, 43–60

Index

aerial photography 78, 80
aisled building vii, 37, 38, 39, 40, 42, 56, 60, 74, 75, 77, 84, 85, 86
    Darenth, Kent 84, 85
    Glebelands, Harrietsham, Kent 85
    Hartlip, Kent 84
    Meonstoke, Hampshire 85
    the Mount, Maidstone, Kent 84, 85
    Thurnham, Kent 84, 85
    West Blatchington, Hove, Sussex 85
    Wilmington, Kent 84
Alcester, Warwickshire
    germinated grain 74
All Cannings Cross, Wiltshire
    human skulls 33
amphibian bone 25
animal bone
    butchery 35, 68, 70
    calf burial 25, 33, 71
    cattle 19, 40, 67, 68, 70, 81
    dog 33, 40, 67, 68, 70, 71
        burial 33
        skinning 33, 70
    horn 68
    horse 19, 40, 59, 67, 68, 69, 70, 81
        burial 34–5, 36, 41, 42, 59
        pulmonary infection 69
    pig 40, 67, 68, 70
    sheep 33, 67, 68, 70, 81
    sheep/goat 19, 21, 67

barley (*see* cereals)
basilican building 84, 85
    Meonstoke, Hampshire 85
Beechbrook Wood (*see* Saltwood, Kent)
Bigbury, Kent (*see* hillfort)
bird bone 21, 25
Black Patch, East Sussex
    cereal remains 71
blade (*see* iron objects)
bone (*see* animal bone, human bone)
brewing vii, 40, 86
Bridge–Barham by-pass, Kent
    settlement 78, 79
Broadstairs, Kent
    Dumpton Gap (*see also* enclosures)
        pottery 46, 47, 49, 50, 52, 53, 79
    North Foreland (*see* enclosures)

    South Dumpton Down (*see* enclosures)
bronzeworking (*see* metalworking)
brooch 63, 84
    La Tène I 23, 33, 63, 64, 80
    La Tène III 35, 41, 63, 64
burial 64, 77, 78, 82, 83
    calf (*see* animal bone)
    child vii, 33, 34, 36, 41, 81
    cremation 27, 33, 41
    dog (*see* animal bone) 33
    horse (*see* animal bone)
    juvenile 34, 81
burnt mound 29
butchery (*see* animal bone)

calf (*see* animal bone)
Canterbury (*Durovernum Cantiacorum*), Kent 82
    Roman pottery 56, 58, 59
Castle Hill (*see* Folkestone, Kent)
cereals 41, 75, 81, 86
    barley 19, 25, 40, 42, 71, 72, 73, 74, 75, 81, 86
    chaff 19, 21, 23, 25, 27, 33, 34, 35, 37, 40, 41, 42, 71, 74, 75, 81, 86
    charred 19, 21, 23, 25, 27, 33, 34, 35, 37, 40, 42, 71, 73, 77, 86
    oats 71, 72
    wheat 40, 42
        emmer 71, 72, 73
        spelt 19, 25, 40, 42, 71, 72, 73, 74, 75, 81, 86
cereal processing vii, 25, 27, 37, 40, 74, 81, 86
chaff (*see* cereals)
Chanctonbury Ring, Sussex
    prehistoric pottery 47, 49
Church Whitfield, near Dover, Kent
    Iron Age settlement 79
Cliffe, Kent
    Roman pottery production 57
clinker (*see* metalworking)
Colchester, Essex
    small finds 63
Cold Kitchen Hill, Wiltshire
    La Tène I brooch 63
coleoptiles 72, 73, 74, 75
Cooling, Kent
    Roman pottery production 57
copper alloy objects 63
    brooch 64
    ring 64